ETHNIC CHRONOLOGY SERIES
NUMBER 19

The Romanians in America
1748 -1974
A Chronology & Fact Book

Compiled and edited by
Vladimir Wertsman

1975
OCEANA PUBLICATIONS, INC.
DOBBS FERRY, NEW YORK

Library of Congress Cataloging in Publication Data

Wertsman, Vladimir, 1929-
  The Romanians in America, 1748-1974.

  Ethnic chronology series; no. 19.
  Bibliography: p.
  Includes index.
  1. Romanian Americans. I. Title. II. Series.
E184.R8W47   973'.04'59   75-11506
ISBN 0-379-00518-2

Manufactured in the United States of America

TABLE OF CONTENTS

Walt Whitman believed that America is not just a nation, but a "teaming of nations". This had certainly been true in the great poet's time, and it is still true in our time, because despite the continuous effects of the "melting pot" phenomenon, America remains a multi-ethnic society. Each ethnic group, whether big or small, brought a specific heritage, made its own contributions, and helped in building America what it is today. For any American it is, therefore, essential to understand not only the contributions of one's own heritage, but also those of one's fellow citizens.

Romanian Americans comprise a relatively small ethnic group, and little is known about them, even though their contributions to our country are substantial, and in varied fields. According to the 1970 United States Census, there are 216,803 Romanian Americans, and about a quarter of them declared Romanian as their mother tongue. They descend from an Eastern European country called Romania (91,671 sq. miles, with a population of about 20 million), and from the same people who gave the world such prominent figures as Constantin Brancusi in sculpture, George Enesco in music, and Eugene Ionesco in drama.

Presently there is only one English book devoted to Romanian Americans. Its title is A Study of Assimilation Among the Roumanians of the United States and it has been published in 1929 as a doctoral thesis at Columbia University by Christine Avghi Galitzi. No other book was ever published since in the United States or abroad. Of course, Romanian American periodicals did not neglect the life of Romanians living in the United States, but their articles were published mainly in Romanian, and, therefore, not accessible to those who do not know Romanian. On the other hand, even if some periodicals had relevant materials in English, their circulation was very limited.

A new English book on Romanian Americans is obviously a long overdue task, and animated by this idea, we decided to do something about it. The study that we present in this book is the result of several years of research, and its main scope is to share with the reader basic information on Romanian Americans. It is understood that this book is only the first step, and a very modest one, in the direction of furnishing essential knowledge on Romanian Americans. It leaves a lot of space for much more ample research, as well as improvements in future editions. Needless to stress that reader's suggestions are more than welcome.

* * * * *

The author is grateful for the fine cooperation accorded him in assembling the needed material for this book by numerous staff members of the Brooklyn Public Library, Columbia University Libraries, the Iuliu Maniu Foundation of New York, and Pittsburgh University Library.
Special debt is acknowledged to Mrs. Trude Bartel, Mrs. Marjorie P. Holt, and Mrs. Joan Neumann for their encouragement, counsel, and criticism, and to the <u>Library Journal</u> for permission to reprint an article included in the document section.
Finally, for their outstanding help, sincere thanks are expressed to Mrs. Arline Cohen, Mr. Martin Dooley, Mr. Patrick Fiore, Miss Mara Livezeanu, Mr. Alexander Seceni, Miss Barbara Watters, and Mr. Paul Zaplitny.

Vladimir Wertsman
Brooklyn Public Library
Brooklyn, New York

513-514 B.C. First record on Dacians, ancient ancestors
of Romanians. Herodotus (484-424 B.C.),
Greek historian, described them as "very
brave and honest fighters" in the war against
Persian King Darius I (522-486 B.C.). (See
Academia Republicii Populare Romane, Dic-
tionar Enciclopedic Roman. Bucuresti: Edi-
tura Politica, 1964, vol. 2, p. 1.)

300s B.C.   Dacians led by their King Dromichaites occupied the area that is now known as Romania.

101-107 A.D. Roman Emperor Trajan (98-117) defeated
Dacian King Decebal (87-106) in very heavy
fights, and conquered Dacia. Roman colonists
settled the region and named it Romania,
derived from the Latin words Roma (Rome)
and Nea (New). Trajan's Column (100 feet
high), errected to celebrate the victory
against Dacia, can still be seen in Rome.
Proud of their ancestors, Romanian Americans
often used Trajan, Decebal and Dacia as
names for clubs, organizations, etc.

271-275   Roman legions and administration under Emperor Aurelian (270-275) left Dacia after
167 years of colonization and very strong
influence upon the local customs, way of
life, and especially language. The Romans
were forced to leave by invading migratory
groups and by Dacian unrest.

300s-1200s   Dacia was successively invaded by Goths,
Huns, Slavs, Tartars, and other migratory
groups, which caused heavy damages to the
region.

1330s   Romanians formed two independent territories,
Walachia (1330) and Moldavia (1359), ruled
by local princes.

1476   Walachian Prince Vlad the Impaler, also
called Dracula, was assassinated by political
enemies after six years of bloody rule.
His life inspired the writing of a novel,
and the making of several vampire and horror
movies in the United States.

1500s   In the second half of the century, Moldavia
and Walachia started paying tribute to
Turkey under the threat of losing their
relative inner autonomy.

1602   Captain John Smith (1580-1631) forged the
                first link between Americans and Romanians
                by fighting on the side of Transylvanian and
                Walachian princes against the Turks. He
                fell prisoner to the Turks, fled from cap-
                tivity through Russia and other countries,
                and returned to England. A few years later,
                he sailed to Jamestown, Virginia, where he
                became one of its founding fathers.

1748   The first recorded Romanian presence on
                American soil. A Transylvanian peasant-
                priest called Samuel Damian met Benjamin
                Franklin to discuss some of the latter's
                inventions. (See Union and League of Ro-
                manian Societies of America, Calendarul
                America: 1972. Detroit, Michigan: America
                Publishing Company, pp. 158-160.)

1849   Attracted by the gold rush, a group of Ro-
                manians left their native country for Cali-
                fornia. Unsuccessful in its operations, the
                group finally settled in Ensenado, Mexico.

1850   Around this year, individual Romanians came
                to the United States and later embraced the
                Union's cause.

1859   Moldavia and Walachia united as the princi-
                pality of Romania and elected Prince Alexan-
                der Ion Cuza as their common ruler. Cuza
                was very popular because of his sympathy with
                the peasant class. Some Romanian American
                clubs and women's organizations were named
                after Prince Cuza or his wife Elena Cuza.

1862   Captain Nicolae Dunca (9th Volunteers of New
                York) heroically died in the battle of Cross-
                Keyes (Virginia) while carrying out the or-
                ders of General John C. Fremont. An American
                Legion Post was named after Dunca in Detroit.

1865   George Pomutz (15th Volunteer Regiment of
                Iowa) became the first and only Romanian to
                ever be elevated to the rank of U.S. Briga-
                dier General. During the Civil War, he dis-
                tinguished himself in the battles of Shiloh,
                Corinth, Vicksburg, Atlanta and Savannah un-
                der the leadership of General William Belknap.

1866   Romania's Prince Cuza was deposed and replaced
                by Prince Carol, a scion of the German

Hohenzollern ruling family founded by Emperor Frederick I (1701-1713). (See 1859)

1870   President Ulysses Grant sent an envoy to Bucharest to improve American ties with Romania. This move facilitated future emigration from Romania to the United States.

1878   Romania obtained full independence at the Congress of Berlin.

1880   Romanians appeared for the first time in the Annual Report of the Immigration and Naturalization Service. During the entire decade of 1871-1880, only eleven Romanians were registered as immigrants.

1881   Romania was proclaimed a Kingdom and Prince Carol became King Carol I. His wife, Queen Elizabeth, won fame as a writer under the pseudonym of Carmen Sylva. Some of her works (legends, fairy tales, ballads) were published in the United States. A Romanian organization from Elwood, Pennsylvania, bears the name of Carol I to this day. (See 1866)

1882   October 12. General George Pomutz died in Petrograd, now Leningrad, Russia, in the capacity of United States Consul General. An American Legion Post was named after him in Detroit.

1890   Groups of Romanian immigrants, especially from Transylvania, then under Austro-Hungarian rule, opened the gates for future waves of mass immigration to the United States.

1892   George Zolnay (1863-1949), noted sculptor, came to the United States and soon became art commissioner at the World Columbian Exposition in Chicago.

1897   British writer, Bram Stoker (1847-1912), published his novel Dracula, inspired by the life of Vlad the Impaler, Walachian Prince. The book became very popular in the United States. (See 1476)

1900   Beginning of a strong wave of mass immigration consisting of Romanians from Transylvania, Banat, Bucovina (provinces under Austro-Hungarian rule at that time), Moldavia, and Macedonia (Greece). The immigrants were driven from their native places by precarious economic, social and political conditions.

1901   The newly arrived immigrants settled in or around large industrial centers such as New York, Philadelphia, Chicago, Detroit, Cleveland, Pittsburgh, Minneapolis, Youngstown, Newark, St. Louis, Los Angeles, and San Francisco.

Petru Glafirescu opened the first Romanian restaurant in New York City. The restaurant served as a meeting place for newly arrived immigrants, and played an important role in the consolidation of Romanian groups. The Dorul Society, one of the earliest benevolent, social and cultural Romanian American organizations, was founded in Glafirescu's restaurant two years later.

1902   First Romanian mutual aid and cultural societies - Vulturul (The Eagle) in Homestead, Pennsylvania, and Carpatina (The Carphatian) in Cleveland, Ohio, - were founded by pioneers Ion Martin and Ion Sufana.

1903   Tribuna (The Tribune), the first Romanian newspaper in the United States appeared in Cleveland, Ohio, only for three times to allow its owners to issue stock.

September 13. Farserotul (The Farshart-ian), the first Macedonian Romanian organization, was founded in New York through the efforts of Nicolae Cican. Farshart (Greek Macedonia) was the native place of those who founded the organization.

1904   The first Romanian Orthodox Parish (St. Mary's) was organized in Cleveland, Ohio, by Reverend Moise Balea.

December 11. The Unirea Romana (Romanian Unity) Lodge from Youngstown, Ohio, dedicated its American flag. It was the first American flag dedicated by any Romanian organization in this country.

1905   Romanians of Catholic faith built their first church (St. Helen's) in Eastern Cleveland, Ohio, and founded their first newspaper

Romanul (The Romanian) under the auspices of
Reverend Epaminonda Lucaciu.

1906   The Union of Romanian Beneficial and Cultural
           Societies was founded. It attracted dozens
           of organizations in the following years,
           mainly through the efforts of the tireless
           pioneer Ioan Popaiov. (See 1902)

           September 1. America, the first Romanian
           Orthodox newspaper, was published in Cleve-
           land, Ohio, by Reverend Moise Balea. He
           placed on the newspaper's masthead a famous
           statement: "Published when I have time, good
           disposition, and money." It soon became a
           household word among Romanian Americans.
           (See 1904)

1908-1909 The newspaper America was purchased by the
           Union of Romanian Beneficial and Cultural
           Societies, and became the official organ of
           the Union. In the meantime, the newspaper
           Romanul was sold by Reverend Lucaciu to a
           group of professional journalists who started
           a strong campaign against the newspaper
           America and the leadership of the Union.
           (See 1905, see also 1906)

1909   Three new benevolent societies - Unirea
           (Unity), Avram Iancu (named after a 19th
           century Romanian patriot from Transylvania),
           and Perivolea (named after a Romanian village
           in Greece) - were founded in New York City.
           These societies were very influential dur-
           ing several decades, and had ramifications
           in the United States as well as abroad.

1910   The first Romanian Baptist church was or-
           ganized in Cincinnati, Ohio, under the
           direction of Reverend R. C. Igrisan.

           53,008 Romanians immigrated to the United
           States during the decade of 1901-1910.

1911   The first Romanian parochial school opened
           in Scalp Level, Pennsylvania.

           Publisher George Ungureanu of Cleveland,
           Ohio, started a weekly called Foaio Poporului
           (The People's News). It was published with-
           out interruption until the end of the 40s.

1912   Some Romanian cultural and mutual aid

societies federated independently under the
name of League and Help and opposed the Union
of the Romanian Beneficial and Cultural
Societies. (See 1906)

1913   The Romanian Baptist Association of America
was founded and started publishing the newspaper _Luminatorul_ (The Illuminator) in East
Orange, New Jersey.

Constantin Brancusi (1876-1957), the world
famous Romanian sculptor, was included among
the exhibitors at the International Exhibition of Modern Art, staged in the 68th Regiment Armory in New York City.

Senator Albert B. Cummins of Iowa introduced
a bill (Senate Bill #775) for an appropriation by the Congress to bring home the remains of General George Pomutz for burial
in Arlington Cemetery. (See 1882)

1914   Romania's King Carol I died and was succeeded
by Ferdinand I, nephew of the deceased.
His wife, Queen Marie, grand-daughter of
Queen Victoria of England, popularized the
English language in Romania. Under her influence, Romanians showed greater interest
in England and especially in the United
States, where thousands of Romanian immigrants were already settled.

The Cultural Association of the Romanian
Workers, a socialist organization, and its
newspaper _Desteptarea_ (The Awakening) were
founded by a group of about 200 workers in
Detroit, Michigan.

1916   August 27. Romania entered the First World
War by joining the Allied forces, later con-
cluded a separate peace with Germany, and
at the end of the war rejoined the Allied
camp. Romanian Americans were very pleased
when Romania rejoined the Allied forces.

Newspaper _America_ became the most widely
circulated daily with 10,500 copies reaching
about 50,000 Romanian Americans. (See 1908)

1917   March. At the inauguration of President
Wilson, a delegation of Romanians from
Canton, Ohio, participated in the huge
parade in Washington, D.C.

127 Romanian Americans from Youngstown, Ohio,
formed the Romanian Volunteer Legion and
joined, in a body, the American Army during
the First World War.

William N. Cromwell of New York, an admirer
of King Ferdinand and Queen Marie of Romania,
organized the Romanian Relief Committee of
America for the purpose of collecting funds
to help the Romanian wounded and destitute.

1918   January 15. President Woodrow Wilson received the first Romanian Ambassador to
America, Dr. Constantin Angelescu. Before
this date, there were no diplomatic ties
between Romania and the United States.

Casa Romana (The Romanian House) was opened
by Ambrose Neder in New York City at 271
West 40th Street. Besides being a ticket
agency and a rooming house, the Casa Romana
was a favorite meeting place for many Romanian
organizations, clubs, and even a church.
It closed in 1931.

Shortly after the signing of the Armistice,
the provinces of Banat, Crisana, Transylvania,
and Bucovina (formerly under Austro-Hungarian
rule) were reunited with Romania. Romanian
Americans, like their native land conation-
als, viewed this event as an historic act
based on President Wilson's principle of
self determination of nations. In the same
year, Bessarabia (a province formerly under
Russian rule) also became part of Romania.

1919   Romanian Catholic church and mutual aid
societies federated and founded the Union of
the Greek Catholic Romanians in Northern
America. The newspaper Foaia Poporului
(People's News) served as their official
organ, but soon was replaced by the Buletinul
Oficial (Official Bulletin). (See 1911)

1919-1920   The treaties of Saint Germain (1919) and
Trianon (1920) officially recognized the
territorial gains made by Romania in 1918.
(See 1918)

1920   September 13. William N. Cromwell founded
the Friends of Romania Society to develop
the existing friendship between Romania and

the United States. The Society accorded
official welcome to all prominent Romanian
guests, and published a quarterly magazine,
Roumania, which was the best magazine on
Romania printed in English.

1921   Beginning of a second wave of strong Romanian
immigration to the United States. Immigrants
concentrated around the older centers of
settlements. (See 1901)

Romanian women and young people organized
their own societies and clubs in Cleveland,
Canton, Detroit, Gary, Indiana, New York,
etc., with a view to preserve their cultural
and religious heritage.

The Friends of Romania Society highlighted
the Romanian contribution to America at the
exhibition called "America's Making" which
took place in New York City.

1922   May 1. The Library Journal, organ of the
American Library Association, published an
article called "Romanians in the United States
and Their Relations to the Public Libraries."
The article was written by Josephine Gratiaa,
herself a Romanian American.

November. The first book on Romanian
Americans (their history, organizations, contributions to the United States) was published in Chicago by Serban Drutzu. A re-
vised edition of the book appeared later in
Romania. (See Drutzu, Serban, Romanii in
America. Chicago: Tipografia S. Alexandru,
1922.)

1923   George Enesco (1881-1955), world renowned
Romanian composer and musician, made his
debut in the United States as guest conductor
of the Philadelphia Orchestra at Carnegie
Hall. He made frequent appearances thereafter, both as conductor and violinist, and
was especially known for his Romanian Rhapsodies.

The Curierul American (The Romanian Courier)
was published by Pandely Talabac and members
of the Farserotul Society. One page of the
periodical was written in the Macedo-Romanian
dialect. (See 1903)

1924   September 28. The Club of Romanian American
            Citizens was founded in New York City with
            the aim to promote a closer understanding of
            the American ideals and way of living, to
            make Romania known in this country, and to
            foster Americanization of Romanians living
            here. The club had a short existence, and
            in its place a new organization called The
            Sons of Romania was formed by Basil Alexander.

1925   Anisoara Stan, the Romanian American folklor-
            ist, organized her first exhibit of Romanian
            rugs, dresses, embroideries, etc., in the
            Romanian Hall at Farrell, Pennsylvania. Mrs.
            Stan played an important role in the populari-
            zation of Romanian folk art in the 30s and
            40s.

1926   October 26. Queen Marie, of Romania, arrived
            in the United States. She traveled through-
            out the country extensively, and her visit
            helped to cement friendly relations between
            the United States and Romania. The complete
            account of her trip to America was published
            in a 238 page volume by Constance Lily Morris
            in 1927. (See 1914)

            November 17. Constantin Brancusi made his
            first trip to the United States and exhibited
            an important part of his work at the Brummer
            Gallery in New York City. The success of
            the exhibition did much for the propagation
            of modern art in the United States. (See
            1913)

1927   Romania's King Ferdinand I died and his five
            year old grandson Michael occupied the vacant
            throne. Michael's father, Carol, refused
            the throne temporarily. Carol was the Honor-
            ary President of the Friends of Romania
            Society founded in New York City. (See 1920,
            see also 1914)

            Jean Negulesco, noted Warner Brother's movie
            director, immigrated to the United States at
            the age of 17.

1928   March 10. A convention held in Cleveland,
            Ohio, founded the Union and League of the
            Romanian Societies of America by the merger
            of the former Union of the Romanian Beneficial
            Cultural Societies and the League and Help.

It is still in existence, and proved to be,
during the past decades, the most comprehensive, and influential organization of Romanian Americans. (See 1912)

April 15. Newspapers America and Romanul
(The Romanian) merged and became the organs
of the newly formed Union and League. The
first continued to appear daily (and reached
a circulation of more than 20,000), while
the second served as a Sunday weekly. (See
1908-1909)

1929   April 25. The Romanian Orthodox Episcopate
of America was established by a church congress held in Detroit, Michigan. The Episcopate was recognized as an administratively
autonomous diocese under the canonical
jurisdiction of the Holy Synod of Romania.

Christine Avghi Galitzi published her book
A Study of Assimilation Among the Roumanians
of the United States, New York: Columbia
University Press, 1929. It was presented
as a doctoral thesis at Columbia University
and it remains a classic on the subject of
Romanian Americans.

1930   King Carol II accepted the Romanian throne
after a temporary renunciation of it and
his eight year old son, Michael, became
crown prince. (See 1927)

Professor Nicolae Iorga (1871-1940), the
famous Romanian historian, published a book
on America and Romanian Americans after making a trip to the United States and Canada,
and after visiting several Romanian communities in both countries. (See Iorga,
Nicolae, America si Romanii din America.
Valenii de Munte: Asezamantul Tipografic,
"Datina Romaneasca", 1930.)

1931   Romanian immigration to the United States
declined sharply as a result of world depression.

August 14-23. Mrs. Anisoara Stan organized
an exhibit of Romanian folk art at the South-
hampton Gallery in Long Island, New York.
She made similar exhibits in other places,
too. (See 1925)

1932   May. Mr. Basil Alexander, leader of the
            Sons of Romania organization, published The
            Romanian Bulletin in English to establish
            useful information on Romanians and Romanian
            American life. The paper was distributed
            free of charge, but it ceased publication
            after two years. (See 1924)

1933   Constantin Brancusi opened his second exhi-
            bition, with 57 pieces of sculpture, at the
            Brummer Gallery in New York City and won new
            admirers. (See 1926)

1934   The Cultural Association of Romanian Workers
            changed its name to Fraternity of Romanian
            American Societies and affiliated itself with
            the International Workers Order (I.W.O.), a
            Pro-Communist organization. It continued to
            publish the newspaper Desteparea (The Awaken-
            ing). (See 1914)

            Peter Neagoe (1882-1960), the best Romanian
            American writer in English, published his
            first novel, Easter Sun. It was soon fol-
            lowed by several other novels in which Ro-
            manian folklore and legends occupy a prominent
            place.

            December 8. Mrs. Eleanor Roosevelt wore a
            Romanian peasant costume during a White House
            costume party given for 500 guests. The
            first lady's costume was provided by Mrs.
            Anisoara Stan. (See 1931)

1935   The Romanian Orthodox Episcopate started pub-
            lishing Solia (The Herald), official news-
            paper of the Episcopate.

            June 2. In an outdoor festival organized by
            50 ethnic groups in New York's Central Park,
            the Romanian American group was distinguished
            for its very pretty costumes and high-quality
            dancing.

            Era Noua (The New Era), a Romanian language
            monthly, was founded as the organ of Mahoning
            Valley Democrats of Romanian descent. It
            ceased publication in 1939.

1939   Alexandru Seceni of New York, noted architect,
            sculptor and painter, designed the New York
            World's Fair Romanian Pavilion. He is also

the author of several icons placed in different Romanian churches throughout the United
States.

Romania participated at the New York World's
Fair with several exhibits devoted to its
folklore, popular arts and crafts, plastic,
graphic and decorative arts, country life,
science, industry, music, food, etc. Romanian Americans were very active, and on the
Romanian Day of the Fair, they paraded in
national costumes and presented folk dances.

Following the closing of the Fair, most of
the materials were sent to Cleveland, Ohio,
for a projected Romanian Cultural Center,
some materials went to the Romanian Room of
the University of Pittsburgh, and some were
presented to the St. Dumitru's Romanian
Church in New York City.

St. Dumitru's Romanian Orthodox Church was
founded in New York City, and Fr. Vasile
Hategan became the first permanent priest of
the parish. The church organized a very
good library, a Sunday School, the Cantul
Romanesc Choir, and Saints Constantin and
Helen Ladies Auxiliaries organization. All
of them played a very important role in pre-
serving the Romanian heritage in our country.

Constantin Brancusi made his last trip to
the United States showing his well-known
"Bird in Space" and a new marble sculpture,
"The Miracle." (See 1933)

1940   June. Romania ceded Bessarabia and Northern
Bucovina to Russia, Southern Dobrudja to
Bulgaria, and part of Transylvania to Hungary.
(See 1919-1920)

September 6. Romania's King Carol II was
forced to abdicate and Michael became king
again, but without any real power. General
Ion Antonescu, who assumed the position of
Premier, became Romania's dictator and allied
himself with Hitler. After Carol's abdica-
tion, a group of Romanian Americans formed a
movement called Free Romania with the aim of
supporting the ex-monarch's political aspirations.

Elie Cristo-Loveanu was appointed professor

of painting at New York University. Later,
he joined the Columbia University staff,
teaching Romanian.

Radio station WGAR of Cleveland, Ohio, started
a Romanian language program directed by Rev.
Danila Pascu, pastor of the local Romanian
Baptist Church. Later, two radio stations
from Detroit, Michigan, - WJBK and WJLB -
also had Romanian language programs.

October 13. The Cultural Association for
Americans of Romanian Descent was established
in Cleveland, Ohio. Its purpose was to dis-
seminate information regarding the contributions made by Romanian Americans to the
United States, to help Americans of Romanian
descent to better understand their ethnic
background, and their place in the American
society.

1941   June 22. Romania entered the Second World
War by joining fascist Germany in her attack
against Russia. Romania soon occupied her
former territories, ceded in 1940 to Russia.
(See 1940)

Mrs. Zora Talabac of Woonsocket, Rhode Island,
died at the age of 104. She was the oldest
Romanian American to have died in the United
States.

December 7. Rudolf Piskuran, of the United
States Navy, was the first Romanian American
to die in the Second World War at Pearl
Harbor.

The United States broke diplomatic relations
with Romania after entering the Second World
War on the side of the Allies.

1942   The first Romanian American girl to have enrolled in the United States Navy's Waves was
Miss Floarea Buzella of Glassport, Pennsylvania.

Stella Roman joined the Metropolitan Opera
Company in New York City and became the first
Romanian singer to perform principal roles
with the prestigious Metropolitan. She ap-
peared for the first time in _Aida_ by Giuseppe
Verdi.

March 25. The Nicolae Iorga Seminar was
founded by Mrs. Eufrosina Dvoichenko-Markov
in New York City on the premises of St.
Dumitru's Romanian Orthodox Church. It was
the first seminar of the Romanian language
and literature in America, and it attracted
eminent professors and students of Romanian
culture. (See 1930)

Charles Stanceu distinguished himself as a
pitcher with the New York Yankees.

The Romanian American Alliance for Democracy
occupied a central place in the arena of Romanian American life. The Alliance, embracing diverse Romanian organizations, was very
actively involved in helping and promoting
the American war efforts, and it opposed the
Free Romania movement. (See 1940)

Dr. Ann Dumitru of Sharon, Pennsylvania, and
Dr. Eleanor Botha of St. Paul, Minnesota,
became the first women physicians of Romanian
descent in the United States.

October 6. The Rev. Fr. Myron Benchea was
installed Commander of Post No. 1 of the
American Legion in Wheeling, West Virginia,
the oldest post in the entire country.

November 1. The New Pioneer, edited by reputed journalist Theodore Andrica, became the
official publication of the Cultural Association for Americans of Romanian descent.
(See 1940)

December 19. Reverend Moise Balea died in
Dearborn, Michigan. He was the founder of
at least 20 Romanian Orthodox parishes in
the United States. (See 1906)

1943   March 16. The Romanian Classroom was officially inaugurated at the University of
Pittsburgh. It contains fine examples of
Romanian architecture, furniture, icons, etc.,
and it was designed by Nicolae Ghica-Budesti
(1869-1943), noted Romanian architect. On
the upper part of the door frame one can read:
"The Romanian is like the mighty rock which
amidst the waves of stormy and majestic sea
forever remains unmoved." These lines belong
to Vasile Alecsandri (1787-1851), one of the
greatest Romanian poets.

1944   Singer Lisette Verea of New York made her
              American debut in The Merry Widow, produced
              at the Majestic Theater in New York City by
              the New Opera Company.

              Christina Caroll, lyric soprano, became the
              second Romanian singer to be added to the
              stars of the New York Metropolitan Opera
              Company. The first was Stella Roman. (See
              1942)

              The Romanian American proceeds from the Fourth
              Loan Drive were used to purchase a liberty
              ship, which was named the S.S. George Pomutz
              in honor of the famous Romanian general who
              fought in the Civil War. (See 1861)

              Captain Cornelius Chima, 25, and First Lieu-
              tenent Nicholas Chima, 23, both of Akron,
              Ohio, were the only team of Romanian American
              brothers flying the same plane in combat.

              June 19. The magazine Life devoted three
              pages to movie director Jean Negulesco.

              August 23. Romania's King Michael overthrew
              General Ion Antonescu, signed an armistice
              with the Allies, and Romania became a parti-
              cipant in the war against Germany. Romanian
              Americans were pleased with their native
              country's new position. (See 1941)

              The United States became a member of the
              Allied Control Commission in Romania, but
              did not resume diplomatic relations with this
              country until the signing of the Peace Treaty.
              (See 1941)

              The Romanian population in the United States
              was estimated at 100,000. Romanian Americans
              had 68 Eastern Orthodox, 22 Baptist, and 18
              Catholic churches, and were grouped in the
              Union and League (75 branches), International
              Workers Order (18 branches), and in 56 inde-
              pendent societies. (See The New Pioneer,
              v. 2, no. 3, 1944, pp. 12-13.)

1945   March 6. A coalition government in which
              the Communist Party took a leading role was
              formed in Romania under the premiership of
              Dr. Petru Groza (1884-1958).

              April. The Rev. Fr. Vasile Hategan, pastor

of St. Dumitru's Romanian Orthodox Church in
New York City, published a very ample and
interesting article on the Romanians of New
York City. (See 1939)

Lt. Eleanor Popa, registered nurse from
Ohio, was one of the first American girls
to enter Tokyo, following the American Army.

Lisette Verea made her debut in American
motion pictures with a leading role in A
Night in Casablanca. (See 1944)

Romanian Phantasy, a record with a collection
of Romanian folk dances, played by Andre
Kostelanetz and his orchestra, was released
by Columbia Records.

November. The Romanian American National
Committee was organized by Anti-Communist
Romanians, with the purpose to defend Ameri-
can democracy against totalitarian ideas.
Its organ Lumina (The Light) played an im-
portant role in the Committee's activities.

During the Second World War, more than 5,000
Romanian Americans served with the United
States Armed Forces. The most distinguished
among the fighters was Lieutenant Alexandru
Vraciu of the Navy, with 19 Japanese planes
to his credit.

1946   February 25. Time magazine devoted an article to Theodore Andrica, reputed Romanian
American activist, and Nationalities Editor
of the Cleveland Press. (See 1942)

March 3. Stella Roman, with the New York
Metropolitan Opera Company, won plaudits as
Mimi in La Boheme by Giacomo Puccini.

Gloria Vasu of Highland, Michigan, won first
prize in operatic singing, and a contract
with the Boston Grand Opera Company.

Nicholas Magina of Baltimore, Maryland, donated many records with Romanian music to
different cultural institutions, Enoch Pratt
Free Library among them, for the preservation
of Romanian heritage.

George Enesco arrived in the United States

and started a new tour of guest appearances
in many cities. (See 1923)

Alexandru Papana, a famous Romanian American
pilot, died at the age of 41. He worked as
a test pilot for Northrop Aircraft in Haw-
thorne, California, helped organize the Aircraft Testing Service, and tested planes and
gliders of all kinds.

1947   January 14. Iosif Cristea of Chicago made
his debut with the Boston Opera Company.
He appeared in La Traviata by Giuseppe Verdi.

February 10. Romania signed the Peace Treaty
in Paris, retaining all her prewar territories
except Bessarabia, North Bucovina, and South
Dobrudja. Many Romanian Americans considered
the treaty unfair to Romania. (See 1918)

The movie The Jolson Story featured a melodious "Anniversary Waltz" by the Romanian
composer I. V. Ivanovici. The song first
appeared in the twenties and is known in Romania under the name of "Waves of the Danube."

Johnny Moldovan signed a contract with the
New York Yankees and became the second Romanian to join this team. Charles Stanceu
was the first. (See 1942)

Two books, Merry Midwife and They Crossed
Mountains, both dealing with reminiscences
about Romanian native places, were published
by Eugene Teodorescu and Anisoara Stan. The
second book also described interesting episodes
regarding life in different Romanian American
communities.

December 30. Romania's King Michael was
forced to abdicate and the country became a
People's Republic ruled by the Communist
Party. Constantin Parhon was named president
and Dr. Petru Groza continued to be premier.
Romanian Americans grouped around the newspaper Desteptarea showed their support for
the new regime, but the great majority of
Romanian Americans, organizations and periodicals expressed dissatisfaction and concern
for the future of Romania.

1948   At the beginning of the year, Rev. R. C.

Igrisan of Detroit, Michigan, died at the
age of 76. The reverend was a pioneer among
the Baptists in the United States. He was
very active in community life and encouraged
and helped many young people in the persuit
of higher education. Several of his pro-
teges became Baptist ministers in this
country. (See 1910)

The Cultural Association for Americans of
Romanian Descent and its publication The New
Pioneer ceased their existence. Both have
played a very important role in the molding
of Romanian American spiritual life during
the forties. (See 1942)

The Romanian Welfare, Inc., was created in
New York City with the purpose of assisting
new immigrants and to grant scholarships to
immigrant students.

At the Fourth United Nations Festival in New
York City, the Romanian program enjoyed a
marked success with the George Enesco choris-
ters and dancers of Cleveland, Ohio. Princess Cantacuzino-Enesco, George Enesco's
wife, feted the group at a tea after the
festival.

September 6. The Association of Romanian
Catholics of America (ARCA) and its newspaper
Unirea (Unity) were founded in East Chicago,
Indiana. The Association has a religious
and mutual aid character. (See 1919)

A Romanian scholarship fund to aid worthy
students of Romanian descent was established
at Kent State University, Kent, Ohio. In
order to qualify for the scholarships,
students had to display a reading and writing knowledge of the Romanian language, and
acquaintance with Romanian history and
literature.

George Enesco became a faculty member of the
Mannes College of Music in New York City,
teaching a class in interpretation of music.
He helped and encouraged many young musicians
such as Yehudi Menuhin and other outstanding
American violinists. (See 1946)

November 8. The Cultural Association for
Americans of Romanian Descent sent a message

of support to Franklin D. Roosevelt after his reelection as president.

1949   Dr. Nicholas Georgescu-Roegen, noted economist and author of several books, joined the Vanderbilt University after leaving a teaching position at Harvard University.

The newspaper Desteptarea (The Awakening) changed its title to Romanul American (The Romanian American) and continued to embrace a pro-Communist view. (See 1934)

The Romanian American National Committee was reorganized and changed its name to Romanian National Committee. It adopted a pro-monarchist position, supporting the deposed King Michael of Romania. (See 1947)

December 1. Ionel Perlea (1901-1970), noted Romanian conductor, made his American debut with the New York Metropolitan Opera. He conducted Tristan and Isolde by Richard Wagner.

George Zolnay died at the age of 86. He was the founder and president of the St. Louis Artists Guild and author of many important monuments in the United States. (See 1892)

1950   January 23. George Enesco appeared at Carnegie Hall in New York City in a quadruple capacity: composer, violinist, pianist and conductor. He was accompanied by the New York Philharmonic Symphony conducted by Ionel Perlea. (See 1948)

The American Romanian Orthodox Youth (AROY) was founded under the auspices of the Romanian Orthodox Episcopate of America.

1951   Anisoara Stan published a book on Romanian cooking with about 450 recipes. It was the first time that an entire book devoted to Romanian cooking appeared in English. (See Stan, Anisoara, The Romanian Cooking. New York: The Citadel Press, 1951.)

1952   July 18. Dr. Petru Groza became the new president of Romania, replacing Dr. Constantin Parhon. A Soviet type Constitution was adopted later and Romania officially became a Soviet satellite. (See 1947)

The Iuliu Maniu American-Romanian Relief
Foundation was founded in New York City.
It helps new immigrants to resettle and pro-
vides scholarships for students.

Conductor Ionel Perlea joined the faculty of
the Manhattan College of Music in New York
City where he taught for the next 18 years.
(See 1950)

1954   May 4. George Enesco died in Paris at the
            age of 73 after a long illness. (See 1950)

1956   Dr. George E. Palade was promoted to the
            rank of Professor of Cell Biology at Rocke-
            feller University, New York City. He joined
            the university in the 1950s, published more
            than 100 scientific papers, and won several
            scientific awards for his substantial con-
            tributions to the study of the cell structure.
            (See Moritz, Charles, ed., Current Biography
            Yearbook. New York: H.W. Wilson Co., 1967,
            pp. 324-326.)

            The newspaper Romania was founded by the Ro-
            manian National Committee. (See 1949)

            Romanian stamps. Two issues devoted to fa-
            mous writers and great personalities in the
            world included, among others, Walt Whitman
            (1819-1892), American poet, and Benjamin
            Franklin (1706-1790), American statesman,
            scientist and writer. (See Scott Publishing
            Co., Scott Standard Postage Stamp Catalogue.
            New York: 1974, Romania no. 1076 and no.
            1122.)

1957   March 16. Constantin Brancusi died in Paris
            at the age of 81 and was buried in the
            Montparnasse Cemetery. Besides his monu-
            mental works, the sculptor left a famous
            slogan: "Create like a God, Order like a
            King, Work like a Slave." (See 1939)

1958   Eugene Ionesco, famous Romanian born avant-
            garde playwright, was played for the first
            time in New York City. He won praise from
            critics for The Chairs, The Bald Soprano and,
            a few years later, for The Rhinoceros. (See
            Moritz, Ch., ed., Current Biography Yearbook.
            New York: H. W. Wilson Co., 1959, pp. 1999-
            2001.)

Romania's president, Dr. Petru Groza, died
and was replaced by Ion Gheorghe Maurer.
(See 1952)

Romanian stamps. A new set honoring great
personalities of the world included Henry
Longfellow (1807-1882), American poet. (See
Scott's Catalogue, ibid., Romania, no. 1221.)

1959   Romanian stamps. A set commemorating the
500th Anniversary of the founding of Bucharest included a stamp depicting the Walachian
Prince Vlad the Impaler, called Dracula.
(See Scott's Catalogue, ibid., Romania, no.
1281; see also 1897.)

1960   The Romanian Orthodox Episcopate of America
joined the Russian Orthodox Metropolia from
New York City, after several years of broken
canonical ties with the Orthodox Church from
Romania. (See 1929)

Peter Neagoe died at the age of 78 in New
Jersey. He wrote several novels devoted to
the Romanian peasant, his life, customs,
speech, etc. (See 1934)

A pamphlet entitled Romanian Embroidery:
A Dying Folk Art by Dorothy Norris Harkness
was published under the auspices of the
Iuliu Maniu Foundation in New York City.
The material was appreciated especially for
its fine illustrations.

1961   Silviu Craciunas published in New York The
Lost Footsteps, an autobiographic book dealing with the author's experiences in Romania
after the Second World War.

Gheorghe Gheorghiu-Dej (1901-1965), Romania's
Communist Party chief, became the country's
president, replacing Ion Gheorghe Maurer.
Under the regime of Gheorghiu-Dej, Romanian
immigration to the United States reached the
lowest level (only 1036 immigrants during
the 1951-1960 decade).

1962   Dr. Mircea Eliade, world renowned scholar,
specialized in mythology and religion, became Distinguished Service Professor at Chicago University. He taught History of Religions and published numerous books on the
nature of religion, zen budhism, mythology

subjects, etc.

Prof. Elie Cristo-Loveanu published The
Romanian Language, considered the best and
most comprehensive manual for those who are
interested in this language, its grammar,
etc. He also painted President Dwight
Eisenhower's portrait at Columbia University,
New York. (See 1940)

Vasile Posteuca, a leading Romanian American
poet writing in Romanian, published a collection of poems called Cintece de Fluer (Songs
of the Flute).

1963   Mircea Vasiliu published Which Way to the
Melting Pot, a book describing, with a delightful sense of humor, the author's efforts
to learn English and to adjust himself in
America after giving up a diplomatic career
and embracing a new profession as a book illustrator. This book, as well as a previous
one named The Pleasure Is Mine, were favorably received by critics.

1964   Romanian stamps. A four value set was devoted to George Enesco. (See Scott's Catalogue, ibid., Romania, nos. 1673-1676; see
also 1954.)

Mugur Valahu, a Romanian American journalist,
published a book called The Katanga Circus,
sharing his views on the Congo crisis at
that time.

Jean Negulesco directed his last movie called
The Pleasure Seekers. During the last three
decades he directed dozens of movies and became a prominent personality in the movie
industry. (See 1941)

1965   March 11. Gheorghe Gheorghiu-Dej, Romania's
Chief of State and Party, died, and was replaced by Chivu Stoica as head of the state
but Nicolae Ceausescu, a close associate of
the deceased, became the party boss. A new,
more relaxed policy of issuing visas to
emigrants was adopted, and the number of Romanian immigrants to the United States started
to increase slightly. (See 1961)

Romanian stamps. A set honoring space satel-
lites included American Ranger 6 and Ranger

7. It was followed by another set for international achievements in space, which showed American Gemini 6 and Gemini 7. Both sets presented interest to American topical philatelists. (See Scott's Catalogue, ibid., Romania, nos. 1713, 1714, 1848.)

Nicolae Novac, a noted Romanian American poet, published a collection of poems named Ultimul Invins (The Last of the Vanquished). Novac issued a magazine titled Vers in the early 50s, and later associated himself with Vasile Posteuca as coeditor of Drum, a quarterly cultivating Romanian literary talents in the United States. (See 1962)

1967   Dr. Nicholas Georgescu-Roegen was named Harvie Branscomb Distinguished Professor at Vanderbilt University. This honor is awarded annually in recognition of a distinguished member of the faculty who has advanced the aims of the University. (See 1949)

The Orthodox Brotherhood was founded as an auxiliary of the Romanian Orthodox Episcopate.

Eli Popa published his Romania Is A Song: A Sample of Verse in Translation, a volume of translations from Romanian classics and Romanian American poets.

Romanian stamps. A set of seven values commemorating the 10th anniversary of the death of the world famous sculptor Constantin Brancusi. Some of the works shown on the stamps can be viewed in the United States. (See Scott's Catalogue, ibid., Romania, nos. 1913-1919; see also 1957.)

December. Nicolae Ceausescu, Romania's Party Chief, became the country's new president. A new political line of independent nationalism, neutral stand in the Sino-Soviet dispute, and closer relations with the United States was promoted. (See 1965)

1968   The newspaper Romanul American (The Romanian American) ceased publication after an existence of 54 years. (See 1949)

Jaques Sandulescu of New York published in English a book named Donbass, a moving story

of the author's life at the age of 15 in
Russian slave labor camps.

1969   August 2-4. President Richard Nixon and his
wife visited Romania. It was the first visit
of an American president to this country and
it helped to improve American-Romanian relations. (See New York Times, August 4, 1969.)

Mircea Vasiliu became a well reputed writer
of self-illustrated juvenile books after pub-
lishing about a dozen of titles such as
What's Happening?, Mortimer, the Friendly
Dragon, Do You Remember?, etc. (See Harte,
Barbara, et al., ed., Contemporary Authors.
Detroit: Gale Research Company, 1970, v.
23-24, p. 425.)

Lavinia Russ published The Girl on the Floor
Will Tell You, a book for children, illustra-
ted by Mircea Vasiliu.

1970   January. The United States Information Center was opened in Bucharest, capitol of Romania. It has classes in English, attended
by about 4,000 persons, theater, music per-
formances, etc. Concomitantly, a Romanian
Government library was opened in New York
City.

July 30. Ionel Perlea died at the age of 69
in New York City. (See 1952; see also New
York Times, July 31, 1970.)

October 11-28. President Nicolae Ceausescu
of Romania and his wife visited the United
States and had contacts with some of the Romanian American leaders. It was the first
visit by a Romanian Communist chief of state
to the United States. (See 1965)

Latest United States Census recorded 216,803
Romanian Americans. They roughly represented
1/10 of a percent of the total present United
States population. 146,116 Romanian Americans
were native born, while 70,687 were foreign
born. 56,590 Romanian Americans declared
Romanian as their mother tongue.

1970-1971   Marie France Ionesco, daughter of playwright
Eugene Ionesco, served on the staff of New
York University as visiting instructor in
French. (See 1958)

The prize was shared by Palade with two other
scientists - Albert Claude, Belgian, and
Christian Rene de Duve, American - who made
major contributions to the understanding of
the inner workings of living cells. (See
New York Times, October 11, 1974; see also
1972.)

Dann Sakall and Alan Harrington published a
very interesting book titled Love and Evil:
From a Probation Officer's Casebook. The
first author, who is a Romanian from Michigan,
presently is a probation officer in Tucson,
Arizona. He shares his observations regarding our correctional system.

John Blebea, 18, a graduate of Alliance High
School, was named recipient of National Youth
of the Year Award. He maintained a straight
"A" average and was very active in extra-
curricular work.

Ioanna Salajan published her Zen Comics, a
collection of zen stories and koans inter-
preted through the medium of the comic strip.

December 9. At a reception for Nobel Prize
winners in Stockholm, Sweden, Dr. George
Palade predicted that man would conquer can-
cer in the near future, perhaps in ten to
twenty years. According to Palade, "The
problem is how to make the cell defense system more efficient, like we do against bac-
teria infections." (See New York Times,
December 10, 1974.)

DOCUMENTS

GENERAL GEORGE POMUTZ IN THE CIVIL WAR
1861-1865

Pomutz was a Romanian immigrant from
Hungary, who enroled in the 15th
Iowa Regiment, one of the elite units
of the Union's Army. Pomutz distinguished himself in several battles and
rose to the rank of U. S. Brigadier
General at the end of the Civil War.
Pomutz helped in preparing the history
of his regiment, a book from which we
have extracted relevant pages.

Source: William W. Belknap, History
of the Fifteenth Regiment, Iowa Veteran Volunteer Infantry. Keokuk,
Iowa: R. B. Ogden & Son, 1887.

FIFTEENTH IOWA VETERAN INFANTRY.

HISTORY OF THE REGIMENT.

(Introductory Letter.)

KEOKUK, Nov. 30, 1865.

Brig. General N. B. Baker, Adjutant-General of Iowa:

GENERAL:—In obedience to the resolution adopted by the General Assembly of the State of Iowa, approved February 23, 1864,
and agreeably to circular No. 10, series 1864, from Adjutant-General's office of the state, I have the honor to forward to you, for the
information and use of your department, a copy of a history of the
15th Iowa Veteran Volunteer Infantry, showing, in a connected
form, the part taken by that Regiment in the military operations
during the war, and supplying the deficiencies of the reports of
former years. The items thereof agree with the official records
and books of the command, and each campaign being under a separate heading, the official reports and lists of casualties, diagrams of
positions, etc., belonging to it, are annexed to the same.

The completion of this detailed report has been unavoidably delayed by reason of the constant, active service in which the Regiment has been engaged during the last two years, and on account

of the greatly increased labor caused by the large number of new recruits received in the midst of the last great campaign of the war.

I have the honor to be, very respectfully,

Your Obedient Servant, GEO. POMUTZ,
Late Lieutenant-Colonel 15th Iowa Veteran Infantry,
Commanding Regiment.

RECAPITULATION.

	Killed.	Mortally Wounded	Wounded	Total Wounded.	Missing	Total Casualties.
Field and staff			3	3	0	3
Non-Commissioned Staff			1	1	0	1
" A " Company	4	2	19	21	0	25
" B " Company	1	5	6	11	1	13
" C " Company	1	1	13	14	0	15
" D " Company	3	4	14	18	1	22
" E " Company	4	3	17	20	1	25
" F " Company	3	3	17	20	0	23
" G " Company	1	1	13	14	2	17
" H " Company	1	2	16	18	1	20
" I " Company	4	6	15	21	1	26
" K " Company	2	5	12	17	4	23
Total	24	32	146	178	11	213

NOTE: Without original lists of casualties, it is impossible to make a list that will agree with the number stated in the reports of battles, and, after the reports have been forwarded to headquarters, other casualties are always found.

Adjutant Pomutz states, about noon the divisions of Generals Prentiss and Sherman on the left and front of McClernand's were pushed back to their second and third lines, and before a brigade sent by the latter to reinforce Sherman could occupy the position assigned to it, that division was again compelled to fall back, principally by reason of an Ohio brigade having given way precipitately, by which McClernand's left became suddenly exposed (see McClernand's report to General Grant, April 24, '62), in addition to his right already being so.

Among the officers of the Regiment most conspicuous for their gallant conduct Colonel Reid stands foremost. He displayed an iron energy equal to the emergency of the situation, inciting the men to stand their ground and imparting his contempt of danger to the entire command. He received a severe wound in the back of the neck, the ball passing through close to the jugular vein, and although paralyzed by it, he fell from his horse, he soon was seen remounted and continued in command through the remainder of the fight.

Major Belknap and Adjutant Pomutz, both also mounted, were on hand wherever their presence was required along the line, keeping the men deployed whenever there was a tendency on their part to collect into groups, and exhorting the same that instead of firing too rapidly they deliver their fire with steady and deliberate aim. Both were wounded—the Major in the back of his shoulder and his horse shot under him, the Adjutant receiving towards the end of the fight a severe wound in the left thigh; continued on horseback until weakened by loss of blood he was thrown by his horse

RECAPITULATION.

	Killed.	Mortally Wounded.	Wounded.	Total Wounded.	Missing.	Total Casualties.
Field and staff			2	2		2
Non-Commissioned Staff			1	1		1
" A " Company	1		6	6		7
" B " Company		3	3	6	1	7
" C " Company	5	1	7	8	9	22
" D " Company			8	8	1	9
" E " Company		1	7	8	2	10
" F " Company	2	2	7	9	1	12
" G " Company	2	1	12	13	2	17
" H " Company			3	3	2	5
" I " Company			8	8		8
" K " Company	3		6	6		9
Total	13	8	70	78	18	109

Adjutant Pomutz writes: In expectation of the attack from the west, the line of the division was formed early on the 3d of October from a point north of the railroad to Battery F, south and facing west. The Iowa Brigade being on the extreme left, the 11th and 13th Iowa deployed, forming the first line, the 15th and 16th in rear and in close column by division, the 15th being commanded on the 3d by Lieutenant Colonel Belknap.

Soon after the partial attack was made by the enemy on our left it was evident that the far greater part of the same moved around the right of the line, making an impetuous assault on its front, at the same time gaining the rear of the line, by which a change of front became necessary so as to face north toward the line of railroad. The 15th and 16th Iowa took position on a ridge running parallel with the railroad, being deployed in line of battle, the 11th and 13th retaining their former positions until 3 p. m., when the skirmish line along the railroad was gradually being driven in, and the sound of volleys of musketry further on the right evidenced the fact that the enemy had gained the ground north of the railroad, and was nearly reaching the town, two and a half miles on our right, and slightly to the rear.

The guns of the battery, heretofore doing excellent execution in Fort F., on our left, were at once removed to our right, and an oblique change of front to the rear on first battalion (16th Iowa) was ordered by Colonel Crocker, which would have formed the line of the 15th and 16th to face towards the said fort. In the execution of this movement, however, the 16th Iowa had to contend with an almost unmanageable thick underbrush in the rear of its former line, causing a delay in the full execution of the order just at a time when the slow but determined falling back of the whole skirmish line from the low ground, towards the ridge the 15th and 16th Iowa were occupying, indicated that the enemy had crossed the railroad and was advancing upon the line formed by those two regiments, and a charge could be expected as soon as they would emerge from the dense underbrush in front of the same. The order to change front was therefore countermanded, the line of the two regiments was reformed, as it was before.

Adjutant Pomutz, of the 15th Iowa, having been sent at the same time by Colonel Crocker to bring up the 11th and 13th Iowa to their former position, (towit: at right angles with the left of the 15th Iowa and facing west), which it was found they had left to form in the rear of the first line by order of General McKean. It was too late to execute this order then, General McKean having already taken them away, and having established the same three hundred yards in the rear of the 15th and 16th Iowa, and the enemy having already engaged the first line, sending a perfect hail of balls into the front line. The 15th and 16th Iowa, being left alone on the ridge without protection on their left flank, fought the enemy, and by their vigorous fire checked his intended charge over half an hour, the men clinging to their ground with the stubborn and obstinate tenacity of veterans, and no doubt if the other regiments of the Brigade had been on the left of this line, the enemy had been entirely driven away from that part of the field.

Headquarters 17th Army Corps, Dept. of Tenn., ⎱
Provost Marshal's Office, Before Atla., Ga., July 31, '64. ⎰

LIEUT. COL. A. J. ALEXANDER, Asst. Adjt. Gen. and Chief of Staff, 17th A. C.:

COLONEL:—By the well merited promotion of Colonel Wm. W. Belknap, 15th Iowa Veteran Infantry, to the rank of Brigadier General of Volunteers, that regiment will be left without a field officer, as soon as the order of appointment shall have been issued, Lieutenant Colonel J. M. Hedrick, of same regiment, having been severely wounded in the engagement of the 22d inst.

While I fully and gratefully appreciate the honor of serving on the staff of the Major General commanding this army corps, I deem it my duty to make application for the purpose of being relieved from my present duty as Provost Marshal of this corps, and being allowed to rejoin my regiment.

I am, Colonel, very respectfully, your obedient servant,

GEORGE POMUTZ,
Major 15th Iowa Inf., Provost Marshal 17th A. C.

SPECIAL ORDERS, NO. 188.

Headquarters 17th Army Corps, Dept. of Tenn., }
Before Atlanta, Ga., July 31, 1864. }

VI. At his own request Major George Pomutz, 15th Iowa Infantry Volunteers, is relieved from duty as Provost Marshal of this Corps, and returned to duty with his regiment.

The Major General commanding regrets that the interests of the service require him to lose the valuable services of this officer on his staff, and he takes this occasion to testify to the zeal, activity and ability with which Major Pomutz has performed the laborious duties of his office.

By command of

MAJOR GENERAL F. P. BLAIR.

ROWLAND COX, A. A. Gen.

October 16th, early in the morning the corps pushed after the fast retreating enemy, over roads and bridges destroyed, and marched half a day on the 17th. By orders from General Sherman, the transportation for regiments, brigades, divisions and corps headquarters, were reduced greatly,* and all surplus baggage, chests, tents, cots, chairs, and trunks, were to be sent away to Chattanooga at once. On the 18th of October, the march was resumed, and Lafayette passed. On the 19th reached Sommerville and Alpine, on the 20th Gaylesville, where the troops went into camp, while the 23d Corps continued its march to Blue Pond Gap, 8 miles distant, where the enemy was supposed to be, and where the roads divide, one going south, another west and a third in a northwesterly direction to the Tennessee river; the presumption being that instead of moving south, as information by the farmers on the road would have it, the enemy would move north to meet their allied forces under Dick Taylor and Forrest, then already in the direction of that river. October 21st, the non-veterans whose term of service had already expired, were sent in charge of Lieutenant-Colonel Alexander, of the corps staff, to Chattanooga, there to be mustered out by the corps mustering officers; Lieutenant-Colonel J. C. Abercrombie of the 11th Iowa, and lately in command of the brigade, having left for the same place, Major George Pomutz of the 15th Iowa, took command of the 3d Brigade and Captain J. M. Reid, I. Co., command of the regiment.

In relinquishing the implements of war for those of peace, let your conduct ever be that of warriors in time of war, and peaceful citizens in time of peace. Let not the lustre of that bright name that you have won as soldiers be dimmed by any improper act as citizens, but as time rolls on let your record grow brighter and brighter still. JOHN A. LOGAN,

Major-General.

In presenting itself for inspection, preparatory to its muster out, Lieutenant Colonel George Pomutz (by General Order No. 14) thanked the officers and men of the Regiment for the promptness with which they had always executed and carried out his orders since he took command of the Regiment before Atlanta, August 1st 1864.

GENERAL ORDERS NO. 14.

FAREWELL ORDER OF LIEUTENANT GEORGE POMUTZ.

Headquarters 15th Iowa Infantry Vet. Vols., }
Near Louisville, Ky., July 23, 1865. }

The commanding officer of the Regiment takes pleasure in announcing that the command is now ready to pass a minute inspection, preparatory to its being mustered out of service and return home. It took a few days longer than was anticipated to finish the work, as it was deemed all important to have the neglect and deficiencies of former years, back to the summer of 1863, corrected and supplied; to have the papers, records and books of the command completed, so as to save the interests of the government, and at the same time to do full justice to each and all who have ever been connected with the regiment. As the records stand now the commanding officer trusts that they may prove a real benefit in future to all of the members of the Regiment from its first organization to this present time. The day and hour drawing near when the command will disband to return to their individual pursuits in civil life, the commanding officer embraces this occasion to acknowledge the promptness with which all of his orders were carried out by the officers and men since he took command of the regiment a year ago, before Atlanta, even under circumstances during the last year's arduous campaign, that have called for the best settled habits of discipline, and have taxed to the utmost the energy and well tried endurance of the officers and men. He cannot forbear now to acknowledge that under the most trying circumstances he could not notice any slackening on the part of the men in doing their full duty; that he never heard of one single instance of murmuring when duty had to be performed; that, on the contrary, he had often been witness to the readiness, promptness and vigor of execution, and to the gallantry with which officers and men have met and bravely surmounted the difficulties arising before them; that as often they had caused him to feel proud of their conduct, so they had also elicited, on several occasions, the applause and congratulations of several superior headquarters. He returns his last thanks to all officers and men for it now.

While he is well aware of having strictly enforced on all occasions the orders and prescribed rules of discipline, with a view to secure and enhance the efficiency of the command, at the same time he is not conscious of ever having, in one single instance, either delayed or omitted to see personally that everything due to the men was given them, whenever it was in his power to procure it for them. Any neglect or carelessness, no matter from what quarter, was remedied at once, even if this had to be attained at the cost of an unpleasant situation resulting personally to himself.

He would call the attention of the command to one object of importance before the process of disbanding will be gone through with.

The soldiers of the Federal army who have fought the hundreds of battles against the rebellion just closed, and have endured the hardships and despised the dangers that will ever tax the credulity of those who were not present, have shown an example of exalted patriotism, of paramount love of our country, of its government and of its laws.

Soldiers of the 15th Iowa! Your record was and is a noble one! For three and a half years you have borne the banner of the Stars and Stripes, the emblem of the power and unity of our government; at the same time as the exponent of your own determination to assist in upholding that government and its laws, you have carried and defended that banner through a distance marched and traveled of seven thousand eight hundred and ninety-eight miles since March, 1862. Out of the aggregate number of 1,763 men who have been members of the Regiment since its organization, 1,051 are out, a fearful proportion of whom comprises those killed, the deceased, and the crippled and the disabled for life. Proof enough of the devotion of the members of the regiment to our government and to its laws.

Then let our actions and deeds show, when we return to our firesides, that we are the foremost in obeying the laws of the country we have been fighting to uphold; that in the proud consciousness of having done our duty full and well, we are determined to keep and enhance the good name we have fairly won; that we are determined to let our future conduct ever be that of peaceful citizens in time of peace, as it has been that of true warriors in time of war.   GEORGE POMUTZ,
Lieutenant-Colonel Commanding 15th Iowa.

July 24th, the Regiment was mustered out of the service.
"Of the thousand stalwart bayonets,
Two hundred marched to-day;
Hundreds lie in Southern soil,
And hundreds in Northern clay;
And other hundreds, less happy, drag

Their shattered limbs around,
And envy the deep, long, blessed sleep
Of the Battle-field's holy ground."   —*Miles O'Reilly*.

ROMANIAN AMERICANS AND PUBLIC LIBRARIES
1922

Josephine Gratiaa, a Romanian American
and a librarian, made a survey of Romanian immigrant communities and their
cultural life at the beginning of the
20s. The result of her survey was
materialized in an article entitled
"Roumanians in the States and their
Relations to the Public Libraries"
and constitutes the only material on
Romanian Americans as a group ever
published in the library press.

Source: The Library Journal, May 1,
1922, pp. 400-404; copyright 1922 by
R. R. Bowker Co., a Xerox company.

IN the heart of Rome, on the Quirinal hill, stands the column of Trajan. It commemorates the victory of the Emperor and his legionaries over the Dacians. The story of his triumph winds its way spiral-wise around the shaft in a procession of over two thousand figures. Among the Dacian captives, shepherds are wearing the wrapped leggings, the same woolen cap and cloak, the "caciula" and "zeghea" that remain the dress of the modern Roumanian peasants at home, or of their transplanted brothers, arrayed for a folk dance in an Americanization celebration in any of our cities. The modern Roumanians are the descendants of the Roman colonists and the Dacian aborigines. The matter of costume, as well as language, is significant of the permanence and persistence of the Dacian-Roman tradition in this Balkan people, in spite of Goth, Slav, Tartar, Turk, and Magyar invasions, or Teutonic and Russian influences. The "Remarkable Rightness of Rudyard Kipling" points to a basic truth when he says: "For whoever pays the taxes old Mus Hobden owns the land."

Ancient Dacia extended from the Theiss to the Dneister, from the Carpathians to the Danube. The area is practically identical with the Roumania of today. The population of this greater Roumania numbers about eighteen and a half millions, of whom fifteen millions are Roumanian. The race has been modified by Greek, Gothic, and Slavic elements. One observer says they have Greek culture, French taste and that they chose a German Royalty. The commerce of the country is mainly in the hands of Jews and foreigners, notably Germans. There is a wide gap between the gentlemen and the peasants with no sympathy to serve as a bridge.

Over three-fourths of the Roumanians are peasants. Some authorities put the number at ninety per cent. They are good-humored, sober, cleanly, and law abiding. The percentage of illiteracy among them is very high. Professor Simonescu in *Vitorul*, of June 20, 1920, says that eighty-one per cent of the women are illiterate. In some counties the number is as high as ninety-two per cent for women and over thirty-eight per cent for men.

The *Socialismul*, published in Bucharest, says, in its issue of Feb. 12, 1920: "61.63 per cent of the children of school age are unregistered, of those attending school less than 10 per cent graduate."

Since the war, the Roumanian government has instituted a land reform to mitigate the evils of absentee landlordism and to improve the conditions of the peasants. Formerly, over half the arable land was in the hands of wealthy proprietors. The new distribution allows only 8 per cent of it to remain in large estates. The old owners are to be compensated in bonds maturing in twenty years.

There seems to be a sincere attempt on the part of the Roumainan government to check emigration by making conditions more livable at home. On the others hand, it has resorted to several prohibitive regulations of the mosquito type, to prevent large numbers from leaving the country. Further, it seems that immigrants returned from America have been discriminated against by their countrymen.

The Roumanian newspapers on both sides of the water have taken up cudgels for their respective patrons in this geographical controversy. Native Roumanian papers write long editorials, saying: "Do not go to America." The American Roumanian sheets print piteous letters from disappointed returned travelers, or advise their patrons to sit tight.

While this wordy war wages, Roumanian emigrants and immigrants cross one another on the broad Atlantic, upsetting the accuracy of census reports and estimates of leaders with a fine disregard for anything but their own material advancement.

Roumanians are comparatively recent among our immigrants, and comprise only two generations in America. The 1920 Census reports 102,823 of them in the United States. This number is smaller than most of the estimates given by their own leaders, some of whom think there may be half a million Roumanians in this country. But, all admit that accuracy is impossible because of the number of Roumanians who returned to the home country after the war.

In a table which follows, their geographical distribution in the United States is indicated, and their relations to libraries is shown statistically.

The average independent American who does not need societies to bolster up his comfort or strengthen his standing in the community would say the Roumanians of America are very well organized. Estimates as to the number of societies differ and the number given by various persons in possession of the facts ranges from 118 to 150. They seem to fall mainly into four groups:

The Union of Cultural and Relief Societies of America, (Uniunea societatilor Romane de ajutor si cultura) includes one hundred and sixteen societies, and is represented by the newspaper *America*.

Liga si Ajutorul, (League of assistance) of which *Romanul* is the official organ.

The Roumanian Greek Catholic Union, whose paper is *Foaia Poporuliu*. (People's News.)

The Federation of Roumanian Socialists, organizations grouped about *Desteptarea*. (Awakening.)

There are also smaller societies here and there, unaffiliated with any of these greater organizations.

It is interesting to note here, that in spite of the apparently formidable banding together of the members of the Roumanian colonies in this country, *America* states disapprovingly: "Not even ten per cent of the Roumanians in the U. S. belong to Roumanian societies, are insured, or get a Roumanian paper."

Only three to five per cent of the Roumanians in America are skilled workers according to the statement in Commons' "Races and Immigrants." Rev. ed.

The Department of Education *Bulletin of Adult Illiteracy*, 1916, reports 34.8 per cent of the Roumanians in America illiterate. Those who read, have an average education equal to that of a grade school, or less.

In connection with this question, the opinion *of America* in its issue of April 28, 1920, is worth noting:

"It has been proved, say persons who have studied the social, cultural, and economic conditions of the U. S., that of all nations, Roumanians stand lowest on the level of culture. No people has been more mercilessly exploited by private and official agencies at the time they sought to return to Europe than the Roumanians."

The paper sums up the causes of this unfortunate condition, as: Unfavorable conditions in the home land; emigration of the illiterate; lack of interest in the workers shown by the small number of educated Roumanians in this country; the indifference of illiterates toward going to schools in the United States; their intention to return to Roumania as soon as it is financially profitable.

Very few Roumanians bring their families over or intend to establish themselves here permanently. The number of American citizens among them is small.

Most of the Roumanians are Greek Orthodox under the direction of the Metropolitan at Bucharest. There are churches of this denomination in Akron, Alliance, Canton, Cleveland, Dayton, Lorain, Warren, Youngstown, and East Youngstown, Ohio; Detroit, Mich.; Trenton, N. J.; Erie, Farrell, McKeesport, and Mount Union, Pa.; Aurora and Chicago, Ill.; Buffalo, and New York City; Gary, Indiana Harbor, Indianapolis, and Terre Haute, Ind.; St. Paul, Minn.; Omaha, Neb.; and Woonsocket, R. I.

Besides these congregations, there are a number of churches of Roumanian Greek Catholics in this country. These are located in Alliance, Canton, Cleveland and Youngstown, Ohio; Farrell and Scalp Level, Pa.; Trenton, N. J.; Aurora, Ill.; Gary, East Chicago, Indiana Harbor, and Indianapolis, Ind.

There are Roumanian Baptist churches in Akron and Warren, Ohio.

In St. Louis, the Roumanians attend the Serbian Orthodox Church.

Roumanian newspapers mention schools in Alliance and Youngstown, Ohio, and Farrell, Pa., at which Roumanian is taught the children.

Roumanian workers in the United States are sober, thrifty and kind hearted. They are proud of their Roman descent, but unlike some other groups among our immigrants, they have not

Stalky's habit of dramatic or picturesque "gloating." The majority of them are factory or foundry workers. Their largest colonies, in the iron and steel manufacturing centers of the middle west, prove their gravitation toward these occupations. Others are in the automobile and rubber industries. Some are found in the railroad and construction work and in mines. There are a few Roumanian farmers in the United States, and a small colony of Roumanian shepherds is in Montana.

It can be easily seen from these facts that Roumanians have not the natural affinity for books and reading that some of the other groups of our immigrants display. Their natural choice of amusement seems to be gymnastics and dancing, and the social gatherings and entertainments that their own clubs and societies supply. Their native folk dances are beautiful and a joy to any spectator as well as recreation for the participants.

The statistics of library use in the table appended concluding this paper would seem to prove that the character of the work in which most of the Roumanians are engaged and the large percentage of illiteracy among them, have combined to keep the number of Roumanian users of public libraries very small.

Romanul in the number of October 24, 1920, says: "Roumanian libraries in Roumanian Clubs are neglected. Roumanians in America read very little. The number of newspaper readers is insignificant."

There has been a real effort on the part of the leaders in the group to improve this condition as can be shown in the generous gifts of the Mauriciu Blank Fund of the Roumanian Educational Bureau, New York, to native clubs and to interested public libraries.

Public libraries on the whole have done so far very little for the Roumanians in the way of supplying books for them in their own language. In compiling the statistics for the table appended circular letters were sent to all the libraries which could be located, and to several State Commissions. Most of the libraries speak of donations of the Roumanian Educational Bureau as constituting the bulk of their collections. One library reports that it does not buy any foreign literature in the original. One of the State Commissions writes that several of the libraries, in the part of the state which contains the largest number of Roumanians, have withdrawn all books in foreign languages from their shelves.

The table further shows that twenty out of forty-four libraries have no Roumanian books on their shelves. In no one library is the circulation of Roumanian books large. The New Jersey State Library Commission owns a small Roumanian collection, and circulated several thousand volumes in the small towns of the state. This seems to be the largest issue noted, but it will be seen, on examination, that many libraries cannot give definite data, so that comparisons are not entirely safe.

The consensus of opinion given by various librarians as to how to "catch your rabbit," seems to be that propinquity is the largest factor in attracting the individual Roumanian to the library. English classes in library buildings, and cooperation with their influential leaders or their priests are the normal methods of securing the interest of any group of them. The Roumanian press is always ready to urge its readers and the members of the multiple societies to use public libraries. The same good and tried methods of securing foreign readers of any group can be used successfully with Roumanians, and a patient ear and good memory for personal preferences, ailments or interests will do much to keep them individually loyal.

It has been very hard to get any expression of opinion from librarians as to any peculiarities in the literary taste of Roumanian readers, especially of those who can use English books. Those who have commented on this topic, at all, say that Roumanians read adventure and detective stories, just as any average patron of similar culture reads, be he foreign or American. The more ambitious and less secure of them keep at their spellers, histories, and arithmetics, as do all students and strugglers with the intricacies of English and first papers.

One notable exception comes to my mind of a Roumanian giant who reads Hamlet, and Cicero and Homer in English for pleasure. But this same high brow once confided to me that Karl May's adventure stories were "Oh! some good!" He, too, is human in spite of his bulk.

Naturally, the Roumanians prefer their own literature to anything else. Here, their taste seems to be for folk lore, poetry and drama. Probably the adaptability of these forms for entertainments and national celebrations is a large factor in their choice. Another determinant is the meagre character of Roumanian collections in public libraries, which, as a rule, do not contain books in all classes.

The Roumanian language is a mixture of Latin with Dacian, influenced by Slavic and Greek. It is the same in the old Roumainian Kingdom and in the lately acquired provinces. Dialects are not numerous and are of little importance. The grammar of the language is Latin. In the sixteenth century, Antonio Bonfinius pointed out that the Roman elements are more ancient in Roumanian and closer to the forms of the original Latin than the corresponding Italian, French or Spanish.

Like other Balkan nations, Roumania has a

vocal as well as a written literature. Its folk lore and epics are not so rich as the Serbian, but they compare favorably with the Bulgarian. In all these literatures, there is a parallel development. It is not a borrowing but a likeness due to similar influences on conditions prevailing thruout the whole peninsula.

These are the divisions of the Roumanian spoken literature: doine, lyric songs; balade, epic songs, which are much like the Serb hero tales; hore, dance songs; colinde, carols; vorbe, proverbs; basme, fairy tales (and here there is a resemblance to the eerie ghostlike stories of the Irish and Scotch) and animal stories in which the dramatis personæ have the distinctive character of that clever creature in Uncle Remus. Finally, there are snoave, anecdotes; and ghiciloare, riddles.

Alecsandri, the pride of Roumanian lovers of poetry, was one of the first authors to collect this folk lore. The most important collection is that of Ispirescu.

Dr. M. Gaster's "Roumanian Bird and Beast Stories" (London, Sidgwick and Jackson, 1915, 10s. 6d.) contains a large number of animal tales, in which God, the devil, and the saints, animals which assume human shape, and human beings who are changed into beasts take parts in exciting or weird dramas. The Foreign Division of the Young Women's Christian Association of New York kindly sent me a translation of an article from the "Steana Noastra si Romana Nova," New York, January 1920, by Feliciu Vexler, which contains a number of little known stories.

Roumanian written literature can be divided, like Ancient Gaul, roughly into three parts, which correspond to the Slavic and Greek periods of influence, and the final one of national consciousness.

The earliest writings are Slavic and are practically all religious. The Greek period, 1710-1830, when the Turks ruled by means of the Phanariot families, consists largely of poems and chronicles which try to prove the Latin origin of the people. One of these early writers, Eliade Radulescu, was the main factor in the Latinization of the written language. He freed it from the Slavic alphabet.

Modern Roumanian literature is mainly concerned with the cultural struggle of the old and new Roumania, between its oriental and occidental elements. Some of it marks the difference between the old patriarchalism and the bravado veneer polish of the over-modernized city dwellers. Pessimism colors the work of Eminescu, Delavancea, Caragiale and Vlahuta. Cosbuc, the Transylvanian, represents a more optimistic and entirely Roumanian tradition.

Charles Upson Clark's "Greater Roumania" (Dodd, Mead, 1922) contains a most helpful and illuminating chapter on modern Roumanian literature.

Conscience, thrift, and critical sense, three prosy, flat-footed, and obviously useful sisters, recommend a practical survey of publishers and book sellers before the purchase of Roumanian books be undertaken. After a year's angling for facts, the following have been secured.

Mr. Leon Feraru, president of the Roumanian Educational Bureau, which has already been mentioned, says there are no Roumanian publishers in America, and there is no critical information on hand which would evaluate the wares of the sellers of Roumanian books in this country.

The Foreign Division of the Young Women's Christian Association in New York furnished the names of five book dealers, but on writing for lists of books on hand at present, only one reply was received. It was from the Biblioteca Romana, 72 Greenwich St., New York City.

Mr. P. Axelrad is the proprietor. His catalog contains a few books on useful arts, some grammars, a few song books, a considerable number of plays and monologues, as well as general Roumanian literature and a few translations. The catalog gives prices in American money, but does not state whether or not any of the books are bound. Judging from the low prices quoted, it would appear most of the books listed are in paper covers. I have not had an opportunity to examine any of the books personally, so cannot report on paper, type, or other physical qualities.

The following Roumanian newspapers are published in the United States:

America. Roumanian Independent Daily, 5705 Detroit Ave., Cleveland. $3. Editor Joan Jivi Banateanul. Official organ of Roumanian Beneficial and Cultural Society.

Desteaptate Romane. Weekly, 1115 East 72nd St., New York. Editor Jancu Roman.

Desteptarea. Roumanian Socialist Weekly, 1037 Russel St., Detroit. $1.50.

Foaia Poporului. Religious Tri-weekly, 1338 West 64th St., Cleveland. $3. Editor George M. Ungureanu.

Romanul. Independent Semi-weekly, 524 Market St., Youngstown, O. $3.

Steana Noastra. Roumanian Weekly, 72 Greenwich St., New York. $2.50. Editor P. Axelrad.

The following list of monthlies and dailies published in Roumania have been recommended by Mr. Leon Feraru, the Director of the Roumanian Educational Bureau. The magazines are of a literary character:

Adevarul Literar si Artistic. Weekly. Adevarul Pub. Co., Strada Sarindar, Bucharest. 80 lei, a year.

Gandiera. Semi-monthly. Cezar Petrescu and D. I. Cucu, editors and pub., Strada Regele Ferdinand 38, Cluj, Rumania. 100 lei a year.

Viata Noua. Monthly. Ovid Densusianu, Pub. and ed., Calea Victoriei, Bucharest. 100 lei, a year.

Viata Romineasca. Monthly. Viata Romineasca Pub., Strada Alecsandri 14, Iasi, Rumania. 140 lei, a year.

The following dailies are "independent organs of information, with slight tinges of party sympathies. There is none of religious character among them." Subscriptions are 400 lei per year:

Dacia. Dacia Pub. Co., Bucharest.
Dimineata. Adevarul Pub. Co., Strada Sarindar, Bucharest.
Izbanda. Teparul Romanesc Pub. Co., Strada Sarindar, Bucharest.
Luptatorul. Luptatorul Pub. Co., Strada Sarindar, Bucharest.

Universul. Universul Pub. Co., Strada Brezioanu, Bucharest.

On a notable occasion Cyrano de Bergerac described his nose in terms of wit and rich variety. A less gifted imagination could only bring monotony to a reiteration of the outstanding facts of this paper. It has therefore seemed most economical and lucid to place the relations of Roumanian colonies and public libraries in a table that he who runs may read.

Town	1920 Census	Roumanian Books	Circulation
Akron, O.	569	25	Not yet in circulation
Alliance, O. .....*[1000]		50	Not yet in circulation
Baltimore, O.	459	1	
Bethlehem, Pa. ..	[1000]	None	
Boston, Mass. ...	673		No data
Bridgeport, Conn..	234	4	
Buffalo, N. Y.....	581	None	
Canton, O.	[2000]	None	
Chicago, Ill.	5137	35-50	No data
Cincinnati, O. ...	687	50	No data
Cleveland, O.	4377	261	639 Jan.-Dec. 1921
Denver, Col.	277	None	
Detroit, Mich. ...	4668	50	151, Aug. '20-Mar. '21
Indiana Harbor, Ind.			About 25 readers
East Chicago, Ind.	[3500]	None	
Florence, N. J....	[1000]	None	
Gary, Ind.	[3000]	50	No data
Harrisburg, Pa. ..	[1000]	50	25 or 30 readers
Hartford, Conn...	347	None	
Highland Park, Mich.	[5000]	None	
Homestead, Pa. ..	[1500]	None	
Indianapolis, Ind..	701	50	No data
Jersey City, N. J..	301	None	
Los Angeles, Cal..	927	3	Av'ge less than 1 a mo.
Milwaukee. Wis..	633	None	
Minneapolis, Minn.	1484	50-75	35 last fiscal year
New Castle, Pa...	[500]	None	
New York N. Y...76288		500	3 or 4 a day
Newark, N. J.....	1307	None	
Niles, O.	[500]	53	57 Sept.-Dec. 1921
			18 readers
Omaha, Neb.	288	None	
Philadelphia, Pa..	5645	No report	
Pittsburg, Pa.....	1493	None	
Portland, Ore.....	258	2	No data
Providence, R. I....287		25 ordered	No data
Roebling, N. J....	[500]	None	
St. Louis, Mo.....	1200	77	94 May '20-April '21
St. Paul, Minn....	559	44	
San Francisco, Cal.	765	None	
**Thorpe, W. Va..	[500]		
Toledo, O........	272	None	
Trenton, N. J.....	395	None	
Warren, O.	[500]	Small collection	No data
**Weirton, W. Va.	[500]		
Wheeling, W. Va..	[500]	None	
Woonsocket, R. I..	[500]	13	No data
Youngstown, O. ..	1375	110	No data

* Where the population figure is enclosed in brackets the actual population figure is not available and the estimated number is given instead.
** Towns marked thus have no libraries.

ROMANIAN CIVIL WAR HEROES COMMEMORATED
1943

An article entitled "Two Romanians in
the Civil War" devoted to Captain
Nicholas Dunca and General George
Pomutz was published in 1943 by John
Borza, a Romanian American cultural
activist. The article has a biograph-
ical character, and is based on important historical documents researched
by the author.

Source: Journal The New Pioneer, vol.
1, no. 2, February 1943.

The first link between Romania and America was forged by Captain John Smith. Before going to Virginia, this gallant adventurer fought with the Romanians against the Turks. It is uncertain how many Romanians came to this country before the late nineties; however, there must have been no small number of enterprising individuals who were lured by the wonderful tales which were circulated all over the civilized world about this Land of Promise.

Historical records show that two Union officers, during the Civil War, were of Romanian birth.

The story of Captain Nicholas Dunca is short. He was born in Jassy in the province of Moldavia. The date of his birth is unknown, and the time and reason for his coming to America also remain a mystery. At the beginning of the Civil War, he enrolled in the 8th Regiment of Volunteers of New York.

He was appointed aide-de-camp with the rank of Captain, U. S. Volunteers, on March 31, 1862. He proved valuable in the battles of Centersville and Bull Run, and the military annals mention Captain Dunca for his bravery in the later. On July 8, 1862, Dunca's regiment was sent into the battle of Cross Keys, Virginia. During this battle, while executing the orders of his superior officer, John C. Fremont, Captain Dunca fell mortally wounded. He is buried in the church yard of Union Church at Cross Keys, Virginia.

About General George Pomutz, we have more information, thanks to Dr. Andrei Popovici, the former Secretary of the Romanian Legation at Washington. Dr. Popovici's story appeared in the January 1929 issue of the quarterly "Roumania", published by the Society of Friends of Romania.

George Pomutz was born in 1828 in the town of Giula. This town is inhabited mainly by Romanians as are the surrounding communities, although it lies in Hungary a few miles west of the Romanian frontier and was not awarded to Romania by the Treaty of Trianon. Pomutz was Romanian by race and tradition; his parents, well-to-do people, were able to send him to the Military Academy of Vienna and St. Etienne, France.

In 1848, he fell in love with a girl of noble birth. Her parents opposed the marriage, but the young couple took refuge in Hungary, where Pomutz enrolled in Louis Kossuth's Revolutionary Army.

Kossuth promised the people of Hungary freedom from the Hapsburgs. Little did Pomutz know at that time that Kossuth meant freedom only for the Hungarians and that a few years later Avram Iancu, the Romanian revolutionary leader in Transylvania, would die as a matyr in leading the Romanian peasants to fight for their liberty from serfdom. Before the end of 1848, the revolutionary Fortress of Komorn fell and Pomutz with his wife fled to Paris.

In 1849, we find his name on the rolls of the Pythagoras Lodge of the Ancient and Accepted Scottish Free Masons of New York. We do not know his occupation in New York, but in 1852, together with his wife and other exiles, he went West, settling in the vicinity of Keokuk, Iowa, then in New Buda, a few miles away. There the young couple at first lived in great poverty; however, Pomutz, an extremely brilliant and enterprising man, soon acquired a considerable fortune.

The first cloud in the couple's life appeared in 1859 or 1860, when Pomutz was visited by a friend from Hungary whom he welcomed with open arms. This hospitality the false friend returned by p e r s u a d i n g Pomutz's young wife to elope with him. They left for Europe where, a few months later, the man abandoned her.

A certain Mrs. Wilson, later a resident of Chicago, gives us a very vivid description of the life of these exiles in Keokuk. She describes Pomutz as speaking a different language, that while the others were Protestant, his religion was Orthodox. These refugees would spend their nights planning a city which they proposed to build on the site of their settlement. The wide streets, boulevards, public buildings would be named after Europan revolutionary heroes. Pomutz and his friend, Dragos, amused themselves by teasing their companions in giving these places Romanian hero names. This proves that his political point of view was different from that of his Magyar companions and that he then understood Kossuth's misrepresentation of "Freedom"; that in one hand Kossuth held the torch of liberty and in the other he clutched a whip to lash the non-Magyar races of Hungary. His companions called Pomutz and Dragos "Daco-Roman", that is, a Romanian from Transylvania, formerly Dacia.

Pomutz, broken-hearted by his wife's unfaithfulness, found forgetfulness in the Civil War. At the first call for volunteers on October 10, 1861, he joined Colonel Reid in organizing the 15th Iowa Regiment of Volunteers. He soon received the rank of Captain. His early military education now became helpful to the Union Army. General William Belknap praised Pomutz for his knowledge and ability. Within four years, Pomutz was promoted from Captain to Brigadier-General, and to the command of his regiment and brigade. We find him in the pitch of battle at Shiloh, where he was wounded; Cornith, Vicksburg, Atlanta, and Savannah. His regiment participated in 41 major engagements.

It is apparent from the official war records that the 15th Iowa Regiment was one of the most gallant units of the Union Army. On May 23 and 24, 1865, the victorious armies were reviewed in Washington by President Johnson and General Grant. General Sherman led the Army of Tennessee, in which Pomutz's 15th Iowa served. Later, General Sherman called this unit the "Pearl" of his army. We can imagine the pride of Colonol Pomutz. In August of that same year, the Regiment was disbanded at Louisville, Kentucky.

In a speech to his beloved men, Colonel Pomutz recalled the deeds of the Regiment and paid tribute to the living and the dead. He said, "Let our actions and deeds show when we return to our firesides that we are the foremost in obeying the laws we have fought to uphold; that we determine to let our future conduct ever be that of peaceful citizens in time of peace as it has been that of true warriors in time of war". His voice was hardly audible when he stated that of the 1113 enlisted men only two hundred and seven were left, and out of 37 officers only three were living.

Pomutz returned to Iowa where, on February 16, 1866, he received his appointment as Consul of the United States to Russia by President Johnson. On May 19, 1866, he was promoted to the rank of Brigadier-General.

Pomutz's work in Russia was described by Mr. Curtin, former Governor of Pennsylvania, then American Minister at St. Petersburg. Mr. Curtin pointed out that Pomutz's activity was beyond reproach, that his letters showed that he spoke and wrote eight languages, and was on cordial relations with the greatest generals and statesmen of that time. During his stay in St. Petersburg, he was promoted to Consul General, in which capacity he served until 1878.

Able men never lack enemies. His enemies in the United States did not rest until Pomutz was replaced in 1878.

Pomutz did not return to America. On October 12, 1882, he died in St. Petersburg. Among his relatives in Romania, a rumor was circulated that he had been assassinated but there is no proof of this.

In 1890, Mr. Crawford, Consul General, found two large trunks which were delivered to him as having belonged to Pomutz. In them Mr. Crawford found a certain sum of money, many documents and letters, and a list of his possessions in the States of Iowa and Missouri. Just what became of this property is a mystery. But his surviving comrades did not forget him; they contributed a modest sum to adorn his grave in Russia on each Memorial Day.

In 1913, Senator Albert B. Cummins of Iowa, introduced a bill (Senate Bill 775) for an appropriation by Congress to bring home the remains of Pomutz for burial in Arlington Cemetery, but the outbreak of the World War I deferred this eminently pious duty.

The names of these two Civil War heroes have been immortalized by two American Legion Posts composed of Americans of Romanian descent. The first, located in Detroit, Michigan, bears the name of "General George Pomutz" and the other, located in Cleveland, Ohio, is known as "Captain Nicholas Dunca".

THE UNIVERSITY OF PITTSBURGH ROMANIAN
CLASSROOM
1943

On March 16, 1943 The Romanian Classroom was officially inaugurated at
the University of Pittsburgh, as one
of the existing 18 International Class-
rooms. The Room is an important tribute to the Romanian heritage in our
country, and has an interesting history.

Source: The Romanian Classroom. The
University of Pittsburgh, Achievements
of the Nationality Committees and the
Office of Cultural and Educational
Exchange, n.d.

"The Romanian is like the mighty rock which amidst the waves of
the stormy and majestic sea forever remains unmoved." These lines
by Vasile Alecsandri, one of the greatest Romanian poets of the nine-
teenth century, are carved overhead in the stone doorframe of the
Romanian Classroom. The floral arabesques cut into the limestone are
of pure Romanian-Byzantine character, inspired by the stone carving
on the main entrance to Hurezi, a famous monastery built in the last
decade of the seventeenth century by Jean Constantin Brancoveanu,
Prince of Wallachia.

The massive entrance door is ornately carved oak. Ample blackboards are set in arched oak panels. These are separated by carved
twisted-rope columns which suggest the Roman origin of many of
Romania's artistic traditions. Ancient original icons from Romania are
embedded in the upper section of each panel. White arva paint mixed
with color gives the smooth plastered walls a blush pink tint. A Byzan-
tine-style mosaic, executed in Bucharest in gold, turquoise, bronze,
ruby red, and black pieces of glass, is embedded in the rear wall.

Four Romanesque windows form an alcove shut off from the main
part of the room by an archway with iron-grilled gates wrought in
Romania. These swing back in folded sections against the plastered
wall. Yellow silk draperies frame the windows and ancient icons be-
fitting the season and holidays are exhibited in the alcove. Through a
special Act of the Romanian Parliament, the mosaic, the wrought-iron
gates, the hand-carved frames of the student chairs, and the ancient
icons which were from the Romanian Pavillion at the New York
World's Fair became the property of the University.

THE ENTRANCE

A massive oak door, set in an elaborately-carved limestone frame, serves as entrance to the Romanian Classroom. Extending from floor to ceiling, the impressive stone threshold is characteristic of those found in ancient Romanian Monasteries. The stone itself resembles in color and texture the Romanian limestone used in the Royal Palace in Bucharest. The door is carved in an ornate style reminiscent of ancient Romanian churches, with molded panels and ornaments that anticipate the carved wainscoting within the room. The wrought-iron level-handle, the key escutcheons, and the outer strap hinges were designed by the late Samuel Yellin.

INSIDE THE ROOM

The floor of the room is laid in square blocks of pink marble which was imported from quarries at Ruschita for the Romanian Pavilion at the New York World's Fair of the 30's.

Also from the Fair came the magnificent mosaic embedded in the white-plastered rear wall of the room, picturing the Prince of Wallachia and his family. Above the mosaic, a painted inscription in old Romanian script tells us that "Prince Constantin Brâncoveanu and his family laid down their lives so that faith in God and nation may live forever in Romanian hearts."

On the front wall and on the corridor wall, twelve-foot long blackboards are mounted in darkly-finished oak frames, paneled and carved in the manner of the icon screen found in Eastern Orthodox and Greek Catholic churches of Romania. The walls themselves are smoothly-plastered and painted a delicate pink much like the tone of the floor marble.

The window wall is finished in simple painted plaster, its only adornment six Romanesque windows. Two small window casements are deeply recessed and have marble ledges. An archway in the center of the wall opens on an alcove with four large windows draped in richly-embroidered silk. Both wrought-iron folding gates across the archway and the magnificent radiator grille came from a screen used in the Romanian House at the Fair.

FURNITURE

Furnished in dark oak, the room conveys a feeling of simple dignity. Romanian peasant artists carved the splats in the backs of the student chairs, creating complicated but highly pleasing designs with a simple pocketknife and hours of meticulous work. The reading desk was adapted from an Eastern Orthodox church lectern.

HISTORY OF THE COMMITTEES

When the idea of a Romanian Room was first suggested, in 1927, it was thought that with only a few hundred people of Romanian origin in the Pittsburgh area such an undertaking would be impossible. However, a small group of eager students, wishing to leave in this country a shrine to their Romanian heritage, formed a committee and asked the Romanian Government for assistance in building the room. One student, on a visit to his home in Bucharest, presented the idea directly to Her Majesty, Queen Marie, and to the prime minister.

Meanwhile, in Pittsburgh, a small colony of Romanian Americans organized a committee and enlisted the help of "The Union and League of Romanian Beneficial and Cultural Societies." This union held a tri-state meeting in New

Castle on April 7, 1929, and elected a committee to conduct
a nationwide campaign for funds. In just eight months, with
full support from the Romanian language newspapers, seven
thousand dollars was contributed by Romanian Americans
across the United States.

THE DESIGNER

Thus encouraged, the Committee chose a designer for the
room—N. Ghica-Budesti, a distinguished older architect in
Bucharest, whose specialty had been measuring and sketching
the architectural details of old Romanian churches.

HELP FROM HOME AND ABROAD

Unfortunately, the Depression and other financial reverses
delayed progress on the room. In 1935, articles began to appear in the Romanian press insisting on another campaign to
complete the necessary funds.

In September, 1936, Mrs. Ruth Crawford Mitchell, the
University officer in charge of the Nationality Rooms, went
abroad to confer with the foreign architects for the various
rooms. While in Bucharest, she had an audience with Queen
Marie and reported that the Queen "will receive and con-
sider an invitation from the Romanian Committee to become
the Honorary Patron of the Room and will suggest the names
of one or two people to serve on a small committee here in
Bucharest, this committee to select a few gifts and to determine the choice of inscription over the doorway."

With the approval of Her Majesty and the help of the
American Minister, The Honorable Leland Harrison, it was
not difficult to form a Bucharest Committee. The Romanian
Room, then, became an important program of the newly
organized American Institute in Bucharest.

While Mrs. Mitchell was in Bucharest, the model student
armchair prepared at the Industrial Art School was entirely
redesigned, and a model section of the carved wall paneling
and a model of the carving for the entrance doorframe
were ordered. To insure the greatest degree of authenticity
in construction, samples of limestone, of Ruschita pink marble and of oak with the desired antique finish were obtained.

Back in the United States, these firsthand reports from
Bucharest, and arrival of the models and of more drawings,
inspired a new National Committee to campaign actively
once more. However, with the start of World War II, ship-
ments from Romania were cut off, and correspondence with
the Bucharest Committee ceased.

Then came the idea of completing the Classroom with
gifts from the Romanian Pavilion at the New York World's
Fair. The idea appealed to the consul general of New York
and Commissioner of the Romanian Exhibit.

University representatives were invited to visit the Romanian Pavilion and Romanian House after the Fair closed,
to select materials and furnishings. By special decree of the
Romanian Parliament, on November 20, 1940, the University of Pittsburgh was made one of three custodians of materials from the Romanian exhibit at the Fair. Mr. Albert A.
Klimcheck, University architect, incorporated these materials
into the Ghica-Budesti design so as not to disturb the original
serene ecclesiastical concept. Finally, in 1942, construction of
the room actually began, to be finished within the year.

THE DEDICATION

Gifts poured in from lodges and from individuals. Romanian-

Americans throughout the tri-state area attended the dedi-
cation on March 16, 1943. Clergy of the Eastern Orthodox
Rite and the Byzantine Greek Catholic Rite took part in the
academic processional and in the ceremony of blessing the
Room. Madame Stella Roman of the Metropolitan Opera
sang Beethoven's "The Worship of God in Nature," in the
Commons Room. Dr. Andrei Popovici, consul general in
New York, spoke with deep feeling of the loyalty of the
Romanian people to the cause of democracy. As a climax,
the chairman, Mr. Pompiliu Popescu, gave then Chancellor
John G. Bowman the key to the Romanian Room.

WEDDING IN YOUNGSTOWN, OHIO
1943

Very little has been published either in the Romanian or the English language about the early life of Romanian immigrants in this country. Because Mr. and Mrs. John Porea were among the first to get married in Youngstown, Ohio, the story of their wedding was described later by their own daughter, Cornelia Porea.

Source: The New Pioneer, vol. 1, no. 2, February 1943.

Two 17 year old girls in Agarbiciu, Transylvania, talked excitedly about the many stories they had been hearing from the few Romanian men who had just returned from America.

Thrilling adventure filled their hearts as they listened to these men who had come to America, made a few dollars and returned to their homeland —rich men. One of these girls was Maria Fagetian, my mother, and the other girl was her friend, Anica Lazar. Each of the girls came from large families, and they found as they grew older that it was hard for their parents to feed six or eight hungry mouths. And so, while listening to these tales of easy employment and big money to be found in this strange, new country across a huge ocean, they determined to go to America.

Maria was eager for the chance, and she was not a bit afraid of the long journey. Perhaps, it was because her two uncles, Ioan and Vasilie Lup would be in Youngstown to meet her, or perhaps, it was because she was young, eager for the excitement she knew would come in this new country. And so, in 1903, Maria and her friend Anica set out from Transylvania for America.

At that time the Romanian colony in Youngstown was small and was grouped about the saloons where kindly German-Romanian people ("Sas") had undertaken to set up a sort of a clearing house for foreign mail and for helping Romanians who couldn't speak English.

This, then, is where Maria and Anica went—to the saloon keeper who would know where Maria would find her uncles. He directed the girls to the boarding house on Poland Avenue. Here, Maria stayed for a short while with her uncles, and a very dear friend of her father, Laurentiu Dopu.

Maria thought herself quite fortunate when a German family, Mr. and Mrs. W. D. O'Connor, interviewed her and decided that since she could also speak German she could start work immediately at the enormous salary of $2.50 a week including her room, board and a few clothes.

Meanwhile, as she made trips back and forth to see her uncle, she met a young man, John Porea, who hailed from a nearby town of Medias, Romania. They saw each other often but when work became scarce in Youngstown, John sought employment in the shipyards of Cleveland. Maria and John wrote to each other for two years. The second summer that Maria was here, the Romanian society bought a beautiful American flag which they wished to "christen." Looking around for a young lady and a young man, who could be sponsors of the flag, the society found Maria. The young man was Nicholas Badila. As is the custom among Romanians, being "nasi" to a child, flag, or marriage, entails expense, but this did not worry Ioan Badila. He and Maria's two uncles insisted money would be no item at this flag "christening", if only she would stand with Ioan as they baptized the first American flag in this new Romanian colony. Maria was bursting with pride as she stood beside the flag. Now, John Porea was proud too, but he was also a bit worried, and decided that too many people in this country were realizing that his Maria was a lovely woman. So, he determined they would wait no longer. He had known Maria two years now, so he proposed and she accepted. They set the wedding date for August 5, 1905.

John was 20 years old and he had recently been given a raise so that he earned $1.65 a day. True, he had to work 12 hours a day, but he was earning more than the other men in Youngstown who were working for $1.25 a day, 10 hours.

Maria, too, had recently been given small raises until now she was earning $3.50 a week.

The morning of August 5, 1905 was bright and clear and both went to the old court house to get the marriage license. The clerk had some difficulty in spelling their names but the two managed to get the license. Since there was no Romanian priest in the vicinity and since the couple expected to be re-married by a Romanian priest in the presence of their families in Romania, they were married by a kindly old Russian Greek Orthodox priest.

There wasn't a long procession of cars from the church to the boarding house. There were just two horse and buggy carriages to carry Maria's two uncles, Laurentiu Dopu, a friend of John's, and the bride and groom.

Maria was radiant in the blushing beauty of a bride, rather than in the beauty of her clothes, for neither Maria nor John had much money to buy fine wedding clothes. Maria wore a "Gibson" girl type of dress with a full skirt, large sleeves and a soft white collar. The dress was white with small blue flowers thru it and her veil was topped with a large wax flower. There was no bridal bouquet, yet the outfit was an "expensive" one. It cost the bride $3.50! John wore his best dark suit. In fact, he had on a white shirt that cost 50 cents. He felt elegant in his wedding suit, for hadn't it cost him $8 and wasn't he among the first to wear with it—a white shirt.

It was a large wedding—some 200 guests in all—some close friends of the uncles—others, curiosity seekers from America—eager to see a truly, old-fashioned Romanian wedding. A close cousin, Theodore and Sofia Coman, were secured as "nasi" — sponsors— and a Romanian lady who had a large extra room (which would some day be another saloon) allowed the couple to hold its reception there.

All the Romanian colony was represented as they came late in the after-noon to witness the young lady and her spouse who were married at noon. Most of the conversation centered about the couple and their chances for success in the new country. They talked about other Romanians who had recently come to America, or who had returned home. For some of the people who had come, it was their first opportunity to go out among the other Romanians. One woman actually wore an "American" coat, and was secretly admired and envied by the other guests who were wearing the clothes they had brought with them, or old shawls.

After the couple were married, they were taken by Maria's uncles to the photographer who posed them end-lessly and took picture after picture of them. By three o'clock, the impatient group of wedding guests caught their first glimpse of the bride and groom.

Among the guests were: Mr. John Vintilla, Nick Tecushan, Nick Roach, Mr. .... Babish, Mr. John Zorca, Jacob Popa, John Stablia, Simon Lupse, ... Jisescu, ... Raftia, Mr. Lazar, and the then prominent John Bozoscian who founded the Romanian Society, and Elia Martin from Home-stead. These men, their wives and families who represented the Romanian element in Youngstown, were the wedding guests.

Romanian weddings are typified by the country's national foods of "tocana de gaina" or chicken stew, and "sar-male", or pigs in the blanket, and though it was difficult to get these foods prepared, since neither Maria nor John had close relatives who could make these and the fine "colaci", the guests were not disappointed.

Mr. Dopu, who had watched over Maria since the day she arrived in America, got up after the dinner and proceeded to tell the story of the young bride, and his tale of her bravery in seeking life in a new country brought tears to the eyes of the guests. He told of the virtues of the groom and promised that both of them would return to Transylvania with good tidings to tell about America. When the "toastmaster" had finished with his remarks, two men set about the wedding tables to receive the wedding gifts for the new couple. Perhaps, it will seem disappointing to modern married couples of Romanian descent who often number their "cinste" in thousands of dollars to learn that these two received a grand total of $92—after they paid the expenses of the wedding. But, this was a surprisingly large amount when $1 and $2 bills were few, and the fifty-cent pieces were easily the majority sums that the guests gave the happy couple. The "nasi" contributed $10 and two other gifts of $5 swelled the total. But this was no small amount when we realize that at the time this was almost two month's wages for any hard-working man in this country.

The wedding guests were being warmed by the kegs of beer and wine and the music of two fiddlers and a clarinet player who had learned to play Romanian favorites. Gay Romanian "horas" and "serbas" kept the guests from leaving early, while a few children fell asleep in old folk's arms. In one corner were the eligible bachelors who were thinking in their own minds, what a fine idea this business of getting married was, while in another corner of the room, the older women were discussing the latest news from the old country.

The wedding gift was all the dearer to Maria and John for already they had seen an attractive table for $.75 which Maria wanted to buy immediately for their new two-room apartment. They used their Romanian tradition of economy to good advantage as they scouted about the neighborhood for suitable living quarters and a few meager pieces of furniture with which to start housekeeping.

This was indeed a wedding to be remembered, for it represented one of the earliest marriages among the Romanian people in Youngstown. Soon, other girls left their homes to seek a husband and a home in America. Soon, the Marias and Johns found that they had transplanted themselves in soils that they couldn't leave. They learned that they belonged to this new country that was giving them the chance to learn to read and write a new language, a country that was giving them the chance to raise a family where each one of the children was sent thru school, a country where John could earn as much money as he was capable of earning.

This was America. Maria and John went back to Romania for a few months, but they returned for they found that the root of their married happiness is in America.

PRESENT DAY ROMANIAN CUSTOMS IN AMERICA
1944

Miss Mary Anne Limbeson of Cleveland,
who had actively participated in Romanian American cultural life in the
40s, shared her views in an article
based on first hand information.
Miss Limbeson attended Cleveland
College of Western Reserve University
and published several articles on
Romanian immigrants.

Source: The New Pioneer, vol. 2, no.
1, January 1944.

When a people emigrate they take with them, besides their personal possessions, their *mores*. This heritage that has come down to them through the years, they transplant in the new country wherever they settle. For awhile the people adhere as closely as possible to their old familiar customs, since they are a connecting link of the familiar past in a new and strange land. Then, as time goes on, these transplanted customs begin to take on some of the characteristics of their new environment. As the new generation, born and raised in the new country, begin to take their place in the pattern of life, the mixture of the old with the new is noticed.

This subsequent merger of the old customs of an immigrant people with the customs of the New World has been evident in the present day customs of our Romanians here in America. This is especially true in the observance of christenings, weddings and funerals. The religious forms are still closely followed, but it is in the social amenities that the changes are noticed.

Stork and bridal showers, for example, were practically unheard of a little over fifteen years ago. Today they are the rule rather than the exception among our Romanians. Either shower is usually given by the *"nasa,"* (nasha —principal maid of honor) some relative, or friend of the bride or the mother-to-be. Many times, rather than have several small showers, one big one is given to which all the friends and relatives are invited. This big shower is usually held in some hall. The bridal shower is often a gala affair. The men join their ladies after the presentation of gifts and with music and dancing, make it a festive occasion.

The religious forms and customs which we still observe closely in connection with baptism, marriage and funerals are always of interest to those unfamiliar with them, and never fail to elicit some explanations.

When a child is to be baptized, his parents choose his "nasii" (nashi) the god parents. Often the "nasii" are the same couple that attended the parents when they were married. If it is the parents' first baby, this is especially so. By accepting the sponsorship, the "nasii" assume the spiritual education of the child in case the parents should neglect this or should die. A spiritual relationship arises through baptism between the person baptized, the "nasii", (god parents) the parents of the child and the baptizing priest; this "relationship" becomes an impediment to possible marriage.

The ceremony of baptism begins in the vestibule of the church where the priest meets the "nasii" and child. He makes the sign of the cross over the child three times, puts his right hand on him to signify that he is conferring the grace of God, and recites the prayers of exorcism. In the second prayer he breathes on the child's forehead, mouth and breast to signify that the devil is being expelled and the Holy Ghost is invoked.

The "nasa," (god mother) holding the child in her arms, faces the West and in the child's name, pledges his renouncement from the service of the devil; the renouncement is done facing West because it is from this direction that darkness and Satan comes. She then blows lightly three times on the child's face so that all evil and wickedness may be kept away. Then facing the East because light proceeds from there, she promises for the child to believe in Jesus Christ and to serve Him. Facing the altar, she then recites the Apostles' Creed after which she enters the church.

Before the altar, the child is annointed with the "oil of joy," which is olive oil that has been blessed. He is annointed on the forehead, breast, shoulders, ears, hands and feet thus signifying that he has become a new branch of the oil-tree, Jesus Christ. Then the child is baptized . . . if there is a font, he is dipped into it. Otherwise, holy water is sprinkled on his head, and a small part of some article of his clothing, usually the ribbons on the bonnet, is dipped in the holy water. Doing this signifies that the sinful man has been put aside, and the new man is clothed with the sanctifying grace of God.

Immediately following the Baptism is the Confirmation. Prayers are said by the priest that the baptized child may receive the strengthening grace of the Holy Ghost so as to be able to confess his faith bravely and to live accordingly. Then with "Mir", or Holy Chrism which is a mixture of 33 spices and blessed by the bishop on Holy Thursday, the priest annoints the forehead, eyes, nose, mouth, breast, ears, hands and feet of the child, saying as he does so, "The seal of the gift of the Holy Ghost. Amen."

It is customary to have a dinner after the baptism. Whether it is a large affair held in a hall to which many are invited, or a small dinner at home, depends on the wishes of the parents. The guests at the dinner give the new baby gifts; these usually consist of money, thus assuring the child of a nice financial start in life.

When a couple decide to be married, they choose their "nasii", the best

man and maid, or matron of honor. The "nasii" are usually man and wife. Sometimes they may be brother and sister, children of the "nasii" who had been sponsors at the baptism of either the bride or groom. Occasionally the "nasii" are not related to one another, but are close friends of the young couple.

On the day of the wedding, the bridal party meets at the home of the bride and leaves for church from there. The groom with his best man leaves first, and waits for his bride at the altar. The bride is brought to him by her father, or some male member of her family. Rarely observed now, is the old custom of the groom going down the aisle of the church with the "nasa" on his arm, followed by the bride with the "nasu."

The processionals, are as a rule, the same conventional pattern with which all are familiar. Since there is no instrumental music in our churches, the processional is made in silence, accompanied only by the sibilant sounds made by the guests congregated there, and the rustle of the gowns in the bridal party. Reaching the altar, the father relinquishes his daughter to her groom and the ceremony begins, the priest being assisted by the cantor or the choir who sing the responses. It is a beautiful ceremony, rich and significant in symbolic ritual which every young couple planning to be married should know and understand.

Prior to the wedding, bans are announced for three consecutive Sundays. This is done so that if anyone is aware of any impediment or obstacle to the coming marriage, he should and must report it to the priest.

The marriage ceremony begins with the priest asking the following two questions of the bridegroom, then of the bride:

(1) " . . . hast thou a good, free and an unconstrained will, and a firm intention to take unto thyself as thy wife (husband) this honourable young woman (man) thou seest beside you?"

(2) "Hast thou not promised thyself to any other bride (groom)?"

After he receives their answers, the priest then blesses the wedding rings and places them on the hands of the bride and groom.

As the ceremony proceeds, crowns are placed on the heads of the bridal couple; the best man assists the priest to place it on the groom's head, and the matron of honor does likewise for the bride. These crowns, which may be made of metal or artificial flowers, signify that the young couple are being crowned into manhood and womanhood, thus becoming rulers of the family, and should live in peace, harmony and purity of heart.

To symbolize the fact that they are to share the bountiness and plentifulness of life together, the couple is given three bites each of a wafer with honey, or sip wine from a common cup. The bridal couple, their hands bound together with a ribbon to show that they are to share all joys and sorrows throughout their lives together, with their "nasii" are then led by the priest three times around the tetrapod and the front of the altar, the complete circle symbolizing the eternity of their union and their obedience to the Holy Trinity. The crowns are removed after this by the priest with a blessing and good wishes.

The ceremony completed, the couple are given a few words of advice by the priest, felicitated, then turn and lead the recessional out of church. They are followed by the "nasii" and the bridesmaids with the ushers. Sometimes, upon arriving at the church doors, they find these barred, and only after the "nasu" has given the sexton a donation are they permitted to leave the church.

It is at the reception, which may be held in a hall, a hotel, or at home, that the survival of an old custom is still apparent. Our Romanian wedding guests do not send the bride gifts, but instead give money at the reception. After the dinner is over, several men go from guest to guest with plates and collect the "cinstea," the gift for the young couple. The first to be approached by the collectors are the "nasii." The amount of their gift is announced publicly, as is that of the immediate families of both the bride and the groom. The gifts of the guests together with their names, are written down by assistants of the collectors and acknowledged by the young couple at a later date.

The church bells play an important part in the life of a parish. On Sundays and holy days they call the faithful to church, and are rung during the high points of the Liturgy. The bells are rung, too, when a death in the parish occurs. Thereafter, until the funeral, the tolling of the bells can be heard in the morning, at noon, and in the evening.

An important part of the wake is the "saracusta" which is held each evening. This is a service held by the priest, who is assisted by the cantor, at which prayers for the dead are recited and the gospel read.

The funeral service in church consists entirely of singing. (Liturgies are held only for priests, or at the request of the deceased's family). The priest is assisted at the funeral service by the cantor or the choir, and the hymns and prayers are those for the dead. At the conclusion of the service, the priest, in the name of the deceased, bids farewell to his family and friends, and asks forgiveness of all whom he may have injured.

At the cemetery, prayers are again said, the gospel read, and after the coffin is lowered into the grave, the priest sprinkles some earth on it, saying, "The earth is the Lord's and the fullness thereof . . . "

It is customary upon returning from the cemetery for the bereaved family to offer food to the mourners. "Pomana," as the offering is called, may be merely sandwiches and a beverage, or a complete meal. But the purpose is the same . . . that the dead may not be forgotten, and that prayers for the repose of his soul and the forgiveness of his sins will be said.

At intervals of six weeks, six months, one year, etc., following a death, the family have requiem or memorial services held after the Liturgy on a Sunday. At the "Parastas," as this brief service is called, prayers for the dead are recited by the priest with the assistance of the cantor. After the "Parastas" is over, a large cake-like bread is cut into small pieces. These, with a little wine, are offered to the people in the vestibule of the church. As the people take these, they murmur, "May his soul rest in peace." This bread and wine, like the "Pomana", are offered to the people so that the dead may be remembered in their prayers.

The present day customs of our Romanians here in America show that while the social customs of a people are subject to the changes that times and trends may bring, these same people cling with tenacity to their religious forms and customs. It is their heritage which they prize deeply.

SURVEY OF ROMANIANS IN AMERICA
1944

In an article called "Romanians in
America", George Anagnastosache ex-
amines and interprets relevant sta-
tistical data regarding the Romanians
in the United States. The article is
based on the 1940 U. S. Census.

Source: Journal The New Pioneer, vol.
2, no. 3, July 1944.

AN inquiry among Americans of Romanian descent as to the number of their countrymen living in the United States would bring answers that vary anywhere from 50,000 to 800,000. This great difference in figures evidences a lack of information on the subject; moreover it leaves room for certain organizations and individuals who claim to speak on behalf of the Romanians to make fantastic public statements as to the number of people they represent.

As in the case of other nationality groups originating from central and eastern Europe where peoples were ruled by other than their own nation, the United States census figures often made—unintentionally—errors. I refer to the fact that before World War I most Croatians, Romanians, Serbians, Slovaks, Carpatho-Russians, Transylvanian Saxons, Slovenes, etc., were grouped under Austria or Hungary because these groups came from territories ruled by Austria-Hungary.

Yet in spite of these errors the only practical and reliable way to approach this question is via the United States Government census, which contains elaborate information on the foreign-born white population in the United States.

The United States census classifies the foreign-born according to country of birth, country of origin and mother tongue. The first classification lists all immigrants, male and female, born in the same country regardless of their ethnic origin. The second also includes their children born in this country. The third is based on the language spoken at home.

The classifications of the last two censuses are based on the political boundaries established by the Treaties of Versailles, Trianon and St. Germain.

Unfortunately, 1940 census bulletins covering the last two classifications, i.e., of origin and mother tongue, have not yet been published. Nevertheless by using the same percentages as those of the 1930 census, a fairly accurate estimate can be obtained.

According to the 1940 United States census, Romanian immigration to the United States dates from 1880. We know, however, of Romanians who fought in the Civil War; most prominent among them were General George Pomutz, who valiantly commanded the 15th Iowa Regiment and Captain Nicholas Dunca, who fell mortally wounded in the battle of Cross Keys, Virginia.

Prior to 1900 Romanian immigration was relatively small, only 22,693 Romanians being listed as having arrived in the United States. During the following decade (1901-1910) the number of Romanian arrivals increased to 62,153 and continued at the same rate for the next four years (27,138), dropping to 4,521 between 1915 and 1919, the duration of the last World War. From 1920 to 1924 we see another influx of Romanians, but since 1924, when quota restrictions based on 1890 immigration were imposed by law, the number diminished to approximately 1000 each year.

The figures prior to 1920 should be larger since they exclude a good many Romanians from Transylvania, Bucovina and Bessarabia, who have been listed as Hungarians, Austrians and Russians, respectively.

At the end of 1940 we find in the United States 115,940 Romanian immigrants, 61,596 male and 54,344 female. The 1930 census shows a total of 146,393 resulting therefore in a decrease of more

than 30,000 which is probably due to repatriations and deaths.

These Romanian immigrants are scattered all over the country, with large groups residing in the following states:

New York	43,950	Minnesota	1,995
Ohio	13,747	North Dakota	1,641
Penna.	10,652	Massachusetts	1,230
Illinois	9,985	Wisconsin	909
Michigan	8,476	Florida	817
California	5,450	Maryland	710
New Jersey	4,685	Oregon	655
Indiana	2,456	Washington	622
Missouri	2,294		

The above total of 115,940 includes

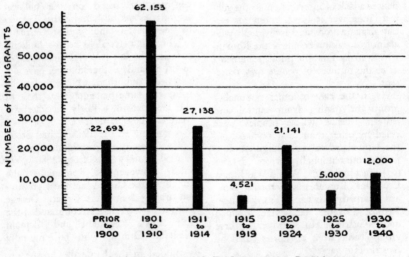

CHART SHOWING THE RATE OF ROMANIAN
IMMIGRATION TO THE UNITED STATES

all immigrants born in Romania, regardless of creeds or races. In order to establish the component ethnic groups and because of the fact that the 1940 bulletin covering the mother tongue classification has not yet been released, we may apply, with certain approximation, the percentages of the 1930 census. The results are as follows:

Romanians	42,318	36.5%
Jews	39,187	33.8
Transylvanian Saxons	22,724	19.6
Magyars (Hungarians)	6,956	6.0
Others	4,753	4.1

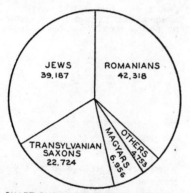

CHART SHOWING THE RELATION OF THE ETHNIC GROUPS TO THE TOTAL NUMBER OF IMMIGRANTS BORN IN ROMANIA.

	Immigrants born in Romania	Immigrants speaking Romanian at home (approx.)
New York, N. Y.	40,655	10,000
Chicago, Ill.	8,387	2,250
Philadelphia, Pa.	5,619	1,400
Detroit, Mich.	5,109	4,500
Cleveland, Ohio	3,997	1,750
Los Angeles, Cal.	2,750	1,000
St. Louis, Mo.	1,650	500
Pittsburgh, Pa. and vicinity	1,500	350
Canton, Massillon, Ohio	1,250	1,000
Youngstown, Pa. and vicinity	1,200	950
Cincinnati, Ohio	1,121	300
Minneapolis, Minn.	1,099	400
East Chicago, Ind.	1,050	900
Newark, N. J.	1,014	280
Dearborn, Mich.	1,000	800
San Francisco, Cal.	950	500
Akron, Ohio	761	600
Aurora, Ill.	750	600
Gary, Ind.	600	500
Baltimore, Md.	596	250
Boston, Mass.	575	150
Warren, Ohio	550	450
Farrell & Sharon, Pa.	550	450
Buffalo, N. Y.	548	150
Milwaukee, Wis.	527	200
Highland Park, Mich.	450	350
St. Paul, Minn.	431	300
Trenton, N. J.	388	300
Indianapolis, Ind.	321	250
Alliance, Ohio	300	250

These percentages are for all the United States. They differ, however, according to states and cities. In New York, Chicago and Philadelphia, for instance, the Jewish group is nearly 3 to 1 in relation to the Romanian ethnic group, while in Detroit, Canton, Youngstown and other smaller towns the reverse is true.

The following table shows the ratio of the Romanian ethnic element to the total number of immigrants from Romania, by cities. Only cities with a Romanian population larger than 250 have been listed.

According to the 1930 census, the percentage of children born in this country of Romanian immigrants is about 100, i.e., an average of two children per family. If we apply this percentage to the Romanian ethnic stock, we can safely say that all together, parents and children, there are in the United States between 85,000 and 90,000 inhabitants of Romanian ethnic origin.

The majority of Romanians came from the provinces of Transylvania and Bucovina, which were under Hungarian and Austrian domination before the last World War. Only a very small number emigrated from the old Romanian kingdom. They came to this

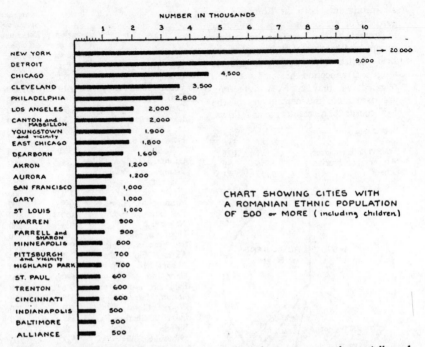

NUMBER IN THOUSANDS

NEW YORK	→ 20,000
DETROIT	9,000
CHICAGO	4,500
CLEVELAND	3,500
PHILADELPHIA	2,800
LOS ANGELES	2,000
CANTON and MASSILLON	2,000
YOUNGSTOWN and vicinity	1,900
EAST CHICAGO	1,800
DEARBORN	1,600
AKRON	1,200
AURORA	1,200
SAN FRANCISCO	1,000
GARY	1,000
ST LOUIS	1,000
WARREN	900
FARRELL and SHARON	900
MINNEAPOLIS	800
PITTSBURGH and vicinity	700
HIGHLAND PARK	700
ST. PAUL	600
TRENTON	600
CINCINNATI	600
INDIANAPOLIS	500
BALTIMORE	500
ALLIANCE	500

CHART SHOWING CITIES WITH
A ROMANIAN ETHNIC POPULATION
OF 500 or MORE (including children)

country in search of a better life, seeking freedom from the humiliations and persecutions they had to endure at home.

Ninety per cent of them are located in cities, working in factories or engaging in small enterprises. It is indeed remarkable how these people of peasant stock, dedicated for generations to agriculture, have adapted themselves to industrial life of America, becoming expert machinists and mechanics. Five per cent of them, especially in Montana, Wyoming, North and South Dakota, are still farming and sheep-herding.

In cities their social life is centered around their churches. This close association with the church is due partly to the inherent religious sentiment of the Romanians and partly to the fact that the churches are to them not only places of prayer but community centers

where they can get together socially and fraternally.

From a study of the Romanian publications circulated in America, especially the almanacs printed annually by the leading Romanian organizations, we find that according to religions, the Romanian ethnic group is composed as follows:

Greek Orthodox	30,000 to 35,000
Greek Catholic	10,000 to 12,000
Baptists	2,000 to 3,000

Fraternally they are organized in two groups: "The Union and League of Romanian Societies," numbering approximately 5,000 members and Romanian section of the "International Workers Order" with a membership of between 2,000 and 3,000.

A n o t h e r organization which, although relatively new, is progressing rapidly and is gaining wide recognition among the Romanians of this country is "The Cultural Association For Americans of Romanian Descent," under whose auspices THE NEW PIONEER is published. This association is interested primarily in the cultural life of the group. Its membership in July, 1944, was 900.

The Romanians are here to stay. They are loyal American citizens and an integral part of this country. They are gallantly and unselfishly doing their share for the preservation of the American free way of life and ideals.

The Romanian (ethnic) group in America has given so far at least 6,000 sons and daughters to the armed services of their country, The United States. The names of 5,000 will be published in the next issue. So far 33 have lost their lives on the various battle fronts.

THE BOARDING HOUSE
1945

This material sheds light on the
accommodation conditions of the
early Romanian immigrants.

Source: The New Pioneer, vol. 3,
no. 1, January 1945.

IN the early days of Romanian immigration to this country (1895-1909) the preponderant majority of the newcomers were adult males.

Uncertainty of the future, fear of the unknown country to which they came and the fact that many intended to stay here only a few years, these were the reasons why most immigrants, including the Romanians, came to this country without their families.

The few men who brought their wives with them soon discovered that keeping a boarding house for fellow nationals brought more money into the family till than by working — often irregularly — in factories.

The average Romanian boarding house was a two story frame building with seven or eight rooms. On the ground floor were the large kitchen, a large dining room and the "front parlor". On the second floor were the bathroom and the bedrooms.

The average number of boarders in a Romanian boarding house in Cleveland, for instance, was around 25-30 but in several instances the number hovered around 60. This meant of course that no one slept alone in the bed and that often there were day and night shifts occupying — in turn — the same bed.

All the boarders knew each other by name and from what old country village they came. "Village loyalty" was very strong among those who hailed from the same community in Europe. Later, when lodges were organized, the people from the same villages or from the same counties usually voted for candidates for lodge offices whom they had known in the old country.

There were two kinds of boarders: those who lived in "company" and those who paid full board, known to the newcomers as "foreboard." The "company" men paid the boarding house keeper's wife $3 monthly, each, for bedding, washing and cooking with the cost of the food divided among the "company."

The "foreboard" (full board) boarders paid at the start $8, later $9 and still later $12 monthly for lodging, laundry and food. The "foreboarders" were considered rather the aristocrats of the immigrants.

The boarders carried their lunches to their workplaces in "pails" which were made ready the preceding evening, except for the coffee. The food pail was usually filled with black coffee (at the very bottom of the pail) two sandwiches or two slices of bread, one pork chop or sausage, one pickle, two eggs and an apple or a banana.

Except on Sunday and Monday mornings, breakfast in the Romanian boarding house in Cleveland usually consisted of beef stew or scrambled eggs and coffee. Monday's breakfast consisted of bacon, bread and coffee. Sunday's breakfast consisted of pancakes (pancove) doughnuts, frankfurters and horse radish and coffee.

Regular Sunday noon fare was noodle soup and meat, home made bread (in the very early days) and pork meat with dumplings. On Sunday evenings the Romanian boarders usually ate sauerkraut and meat. Friday evenings in some boarding houses the usual fare was sausage with puree of dried white beans.

The usual evening meal on other

nights consisted of soup and fried meat or stew. If the boarders wanted to wash down the evening meal with other than water, they could get from the keeper of the boarding house portions of "cow-and-calf," (vaca si vitel) whiskey and beer, which cost five cents for the whiskey and five cents for the beer.

When at home the boarders ate at a long, oil cloth covered table that stood in the middle of the large dining room. They sat on long benches on either side of the table. Before each meal, the oldest man present usually said the "Lord's Prayer."

At the end of each month the boarding house keeper bought a four gallon keg of beer and "treated" his boarders. This gesture, called in Romanian "cinste" was a regular feature of every boarding house. If some boarding house owner appeared to be stingy about it, he soon lost some boarders.

After supper, the men gathered around the long table on which they put a three gallon keg of beer and sang plaintive Romanian songs, the "doine."

Some of the men improvised poetry and sang the words to the tune of some well known "doina." These poems usually expressed great sadness at finding themselves in a strange country, far, far away from their homes and families.

In every boarding house there was someone who could play the shepherd's flute. He was the most sought-after man in the group since he was useful not only at their regular get-togethers in the boarding house but also at such occasions as weddings. The music at the weddings in the very early days of Romanian immigration, usually consisted of a lone shepherd's flute player.

Most of the Romanian immigrants made great efforts to save money out of their meager earnings. Each boarder had a wooden box under his bed. In this he kept his few belongings, often his money (he did not trust the banks) and in many cases, a slab of smoked bacon which he ate sitting on his bed.

When a group of boarders decided to move to another house, either because they heard the cooking was better or if they had an argument with the owner, the moving was accompanied with music.

Whatever hardships the early immigrant boarders may have had, one should never forget the wife of the boarding house keeper. Her job never ended. She did not have labor saving machinery. That these women washed, cooked and baked for 25-30 men appears today unbelievable. Many an American born youngster today enjoys a better life because his immigrant parents worked hard, unbelievably hard in their early days in this country.

THE ROMANIANS OF NEW YORK CITY
1945

Reverend Fr. Vasile Hategan, formerly pastor of St. Dumitru's Orthodox
Church in New York City, is well reputed for his numerous scholarly
writings on Romanian Americans. In
one of his articles, we found a well
documented and ample description of
the life, organizations, press, contributions to the United States, and
other aspects related to the Romanians
of New York City.

Source: The New Pioneer, vol. 3, no.
2, April 1945.

Introduction

THE vast majority of Romanians who migrated to the United States entered the
country through the port of New York. They
first set foot on American soil at Ellis Island,
where they were greeted by Romanian inter-
preters, among whom we find Mr. Pandely
Talabac, who was of great help to Romanian
immigrants during the period from 1910 to
1920. Capt. John Caba, a Romanian, was
an inspector at Ellis Island for many years
and before his retirement was chairman of
the Special Inquiry Board. He was also an
intelligence officer in the United States Army
and a representative of Hoover's Relief Committee in Bessarabia during World War I.

Very few Romanian Gentiles settled in
New York City; most of them went to the
industrial cities of Pennsylvania, Ohio, Michigan and Illinois. Nevertheless, upon studying the statistics, one is amazed at the large
number of Romanians in New York City.

Statistics

Of the 115,940 foreign-born Romanians in
America, 40,655 reside in New York City,
according to the Official United States Census of 1940. This is more than one-third of
the total number of Romanians in this
country.

They are distributed through the five bor-
oughs of the city as follows: Bronx, 14,109;
Brooklyn, 16,349; Manhattan, 7,602; Queens,
2,512; Richmond, 83. Besides the foreign-
born Romanians, there are 44,020 persons in
the city born of Romanian parents or of a
marriage in which one of the parents was
Romanian. This makes a total of 84,675
Romanians and Americans of Romanian descent residing in this city.

The total number of foreign-born Roman-

ians in this country and those born of Romanian parents is 247,700, of which more
than one-third live in New York.

No one has really ever known the exact
number of Romanian Gentiles in New York.
It is very difficult to keep track of them in a
city as large as New York. In my four years
as pastor of the Romanian Church in New
York, I have tried to get names and addresses
of all Romanians residing here. I add to my
list regularly, but it is far from being complete. Many Romanians are "lost" among
the millions of inhabitants of New York and
never participate in any of the events sponsored by Romanian organizations.
their small proportion. Their number is in-
finitesimal compared to the 8,000,000 population of New York.

Among these 2,000 Romanians, there are
about 800 who did not migrate from Romania proper. These are the Macedo-Romanians who came from Pindus, Thessaly
and Epirus in Greece, Albania and Jugoslavia. Even though separated from Romania for hundreds of years, they managed
to remain Romanians. Most of them met native Romanians for the first time upon coming to America, and have readily become
one with them.

Distribution

Aside from the Macedo-Romanians who
did not emigrate from Romania, the rest of
them came from the different provinces of
Romania, especially from the Old Kingdom,
Transylvania, Banat and Bucovina. Unlike
other cities, where Romanians from one province or another predominate, there is no over-
whelming majority in this city from one
province or another.

There are more Romanians from the Old

Kingdom in New York in comparison with those from other provinces, than in any other city in the country. Many of them were merchant sailors, and the others came here with trades they had learned in their native land.

Many of the Transylvanians came to New York from other American cities, especially during the years of the depression. Some of them returned later to the cities from which they came, but many of them remained here. The Banat Romanians came to New York mostly from Philadelphia.

The provincialism of the Romanians is reflected in their first organizations, although there was never any discrimination. For instance, the founders of the "Dorul" Society were mostly from the Old Kingdom; while those from Transylvania grouped themselves in the "Avram Iancu" Society. The Macedo-Romanians organized according to the districts or towns from which they migrated. Those from the vicinity of Coritza (Albania) founded the "Farsarotul" Society, and others, the "Unirea" Society. Those from the town of Perivolea (Greece) founded the "Perivolea" Society, and those from Bitolia (Jugoslavia), the "Bitalia" Society. These were, for the most part, benevolent organizations. On the other hand, there were organizations, especially after World War I, which were composed of Romanians from all geographical districts, such as the Sons of Romania, "Mihail Eminescu" and others.

Whereas the number of Romanians in most of the cities diminished after World War I, the number in New York increased slightly. Between 80 and 90 per cent of them are American citizens.

Occupations

Most Romanians, generally speaking, came to this country without any trades which they could continue here; but the Romanians of New York, more than those of other cities, had some trade in Romania. All have managed to secure employment and make good in their respective fields.

An occupation favored by the Macedo-Romanians is that of waiters and bartenders in the large hotels and restaurants. Their linguistic ability, and especially their knowledge of the Greek language, enables them to converse in many languages and makes them valuable in this field.

There are many prosperous small Romanian businessmen; Dumitru Balamoti owns a grocery store and Mihail Nibi a confectionary store; The Muha brothers are successful florists. Miss Jean Agrocosta and Mr. John Vlad are furriers. Mr. Panta Evi operates his own fur shop. Emil Morarescu and Teddy Martin are barbers. Mr. John Buturuga has a successful auto repair business. Friderich Palievici has recently opened an auto body-building shop.

Dumitru Velikan operates an ornamental metal shop. George Bukur repairs musical instruments and numbers among his regular customers some of the most famous musicians in the country. Constantin Gheorghiu owns and operates a tugboat. Emilian Ovesia is in the real estate business. Pandely Talabac is a notary public and insurance agent. George Z. Michaels has invented a numbering machine for photo negatives which he manufactures and sells. He also has other inventions.

Mr. Nicolae Borzuku is a wholesale manufacturer of women's coats. He has a thriving business employing many workers. Christy Batsu is the owner of a fashionable beauty salon. It is encouraging to note that the younger generation is making a place for itself in business. Emilian Ovesia, Jr., who was recently discharged from the Army after receiving the Purple Heart, has opened a small business manufacturing plastic novelties. Paul Lupie is employed in an important war job.

Many New York Romanians are employed in wartime agencies devoted to helping America win the war. The Romanian section of the O. W. I. was at one time broadcasting as many as four programs daily to Romania. Among those employed by this agency are Messrs. C. Wertler, P. Neagoe, S. Labin, Cehan. These, however, have been cut down considerably since the Germans have been driven out of that country. The Office of Strategic Information made good use of the material available in the library of the Romanian Church.

Among the Romanians working in the Office of Censorship are the Misses V. Ovesia, F. Baditoiu and M. Neag. Mr. John Burnea, Titus Podea, A. Manoil, and Mrs. Dvocenko-Marcov have helped to prepare a Romanian-English dictionary of military terms for the War Department.

Most of the young Romanian women are employed in secretarial work while a good number of the women are in dressmaking concerns.

The New York Romanians boast of many professional men who have made names for themselves in their respective fields. Dr. Valer Barbu is one of America's most prominent psychiatrists. Dr. Socrates Costoff is a dentist. Stefan Serghiescu is a professor of mathematics at Columbia University. Ilie Cristo-Loveanu is a professor of Romanian Literature and Language at Columbia. Engineers and architects are John M. Metes, Serban Drutzu, Stefan Apostolescu, John Edeleanu, John W. Solomon, and August Schmiedegan.

The field of finance is well represented Radu Irimescu, former Romanian minister to America is a member of the powerful holding company, the Atlas Corporation. Mircea Iurascu is the head of the well-known Latin-American Credit Corporation. Dr. Andrei Popovici, former consul general of Romania, recently joined the American Banknote Company. Mr. Stefan Irimescu is with a large investment banking firm. Leon Talabac is a prominent financial adviser. Basil Alexander has been with the Chase National Bank for 27 years.

Among the lawyers are John Burnea, former attorney for the American Consulate in Bucharest. George R. Raducan, a graduate of Columbia University Law School is associated with a firm of Wall Street lawyers. Alexandru J. Lupear, who for many years was prominent in Romanian affairs in America, is an eminent lawyer employed by the government.

Among those qualified to teach, with degrees from various colleges and universities are Mrs. Rozeta (Musat) Metes, Mrs. Cornelia Hategan and the Misses Florence Baditoiu, Mary Nedescu and Martha Neag.

The list is by no means complete. There are probably a considerable number employed in other fields, and the author asks forgiveness for not noting them. It is because of the lack of information.

Restaurants

The early history of the Romanians in New York City would be incomplete if we did not mention the contribution of Romanian restaurants to the consolidation of the Romanian groups. Until the facilities of the "St. Dumitru" Church were opened in 1939, there was no central meeting place for the Romanians in New York City. None of the existing organizations owned property. They usually rented quarters or met in the homes of their members or in a restaurant owned by a Romanian.

One does not observe the boarding house in New York as it is known in other cities where Romanians reside. Nevertheless, there was always an enterprising Romanian to operate a restaurant catering to the Romanians. The restaurant was usually attached to a rooming house, but rooms and meals were separate.

These restaurants and rooming houses have come and gone and have changed hands quite often. Because of the small number of Romanians in New York City and the long distances they have to travel, these restaurants have never been very profitable businesses, but they have definitely served a need. There are, it is true, a number of Romanian restaurants in New York, but they cater especially to the Romanian Jews. The Macedo-Romanians also own a number of restaurants which serve mostly Americans.

Some of the more important restaurants, as recalled by old-timers were Petru Glafirescu in 1901. This is believed to be the first Romanian restaurant in New York. Some of the first Romanians, such as Jean Paleologu, Constantin Dabija, Constantin Negoescu, Constantin Balan, Corjibsky, Figarovsky, Ilie Florescu met here. The "Dorul" Society was founded in Petru Glafirescu's restaurant. It was located on Third Street. Other restaurants before World War I were those of Enache Cosma in 1903, Petru Comanescu in 1911 at 151 East Fourth Street, which was later taken over by George Stanciu in 1914, then by George Grama, I. Du-

mitrescu, and I. Basca. In 1911, we also find a Colonia Romana run by G. Papa-Tanase and in 1917 a restaurant operated for a short time by Ilie G. Florescu.

In 1918 Ambrose Neder opened Casa Romana at 271 West Fortieth Street, which was a ticket agency and rooming house also. Many of the post-war Romanian organizations, such as the "Mihail Eminescu" Club, the Descent of the Holy Ghost parish and others were founded in the Casa Romana. The "Avram Iancu" Society held its meetings there for many years. Through its doors passed many thousands of Romanians on their way back to Romania. The Casa Romana was closed in 1931.

The business was taken over by George Raducan who later moved it to East Eighth Street. Lately it has passed hands several times: Mrs. Paraschiva Kisilencu, Mrs. Floarea Popa, Mrs. Rebecca Vandor, and at present, Mr. Sava Ionescu.

A favorite meeting place for the Macedo-Romanians was the Casa Romana at 261 West Thirty-seventh Street, operated for a number of years by the Carameta Brothers.

Mr. Friderich Palievici is the owner of a restaurant where for many years some of the Romanian organizations have met.

Bank-Agencies

Following World War I, two Romanian banks opened branches in New York City. The Chrissoveloni Bank was headed by Major Radu Irimescu, who later became Minister of Aviation and Marine in Romania and, more recently, Romanian minister to Romania until the outbreak of the present war.

The Marmorosch Bank and Company opened its branch in its own building at 33 Broadway, under the direction of Dr. A. Zentler. It founded a Romanian House, which gave commercial and financial information on Romania. Both of these banks were closed after a number of years of activity.

There were also many Romanian agencies that specialized in sending money to Romania and making arrangements for travel to Romania, such as the Agentia Romaneasca, at 422 Seventh Avenue, operated by Iancu Roman; the Agentia Nationala Romana, at 405 Eighth Avenue: Alexandru Filoti; Pandely Talabac; Ambrose Neder; and the foreign departments of some of the banks in New York City. Since the war began, there have been none in business.

Romanians During World War I

The conditions of distress and suffering were so great in the early part of 1917 in Romania, that relief work for the country was imperative. Therefore, the preliminary work was begun in New York which later resulted in the formation of the Romanian Relief Committee of America. It soon attracted a few Americans who were moved by the courage of the Romanian troops with the Allies and the great privations of the people, and who had great sympathy for that outpost of Latin civilization in the East.

The best means of helping the sufferers was then discussed, and it was decided that sending money and supplies would do the most good, were they sent to Queen Marie. When the committee began its work, supplies could still be forwarded through Northern Russia and some supplies, the money for which had been collected with the assistance of the British War Relief were actually sent in that way with the aid of the Royal Romanian Military Trade Commission. After the Treaty of Bucharest, Romania was helpless and cut off from communication with the Allies and America, but after communications were opened again, the committee was able to continue sending money and supplies. Among its officers were Breck Trowbridge, chairman, T. Tileston Wells, Mrs. Edward McVickar, Mme. Orghidan, Henry Clews and Sen. Gogu Negulescu.

Appeals were sent out to other cities of the country, but most of the funds were raised in New York. A full statement of goods and money sent to Romania was given on August 28, 1920, as follows: To Queen Marie, 43,185 francs, 100,000 lei, 27 cases of clothing, five ambulances, 6 cases of merchandise, 15 sewing machines; to the Romanian Red Cross, 50,000 francs, 200,000 lei; to a fund for war orphans, 326,923 lei.

When the Friends of Romania Society was formed, it absorbed the Romanian Relief Committee and elected each member of the committee an annual member of the society. All the existing Romanian organizations did a magnificent job in helping America and her allies.

Romanians During World War II

When World War II broke out, the Romanians of New York immediately gave their whole-hearted support to the cause of America. Besides the fact that more than 100 soldiers of Romanian descent from New York are serving in the Armed Forces, all the organizations contributed generously to patriotic drives and have made an excellent showing in the sale of War Bonds.

The Romanians, with the assistance of their friends, made a very good showing among the 24 foreign-origin groups in these drives. In the Second War Loan Drive, the Romanians won 19th place; in the third, 9th place; in the fourth, 18th place; in the fifth, 10th place; and in the sixth, 15th place. This is an excellent record, since the Romanians are such a numerical minority in New York.

As a result of the Second War Loan Drive, the Romanian Americans were able to furnish the funds for a P. T. boat which was presented at Bayonne, New Jersey, by Mr. Basil Alexander and Rev. Vasile Hategan. The proceeds of the Fourth War Loan Drive were used to purchase a liberty ship which was named the S. S. George Pomutz in honor of the famous Romanian general who fought in the Civil War. The ship was built at the Delta Shipyards in New Orleans, and was launched in August, 1944, in the presence of Mr. and Mrs. Bennett Siegelstein and Mr. Basil Alexander, as representatives of the Romanian-American War Loan Committee of New York.

The Romanian Legation and Consulate General

The Romanian Legation in Washington and the Romanian Consulate General in New York City played an important part in making Romania known to Americans.

Before World War I, there was no Romanian diplomatic representation in this country, and the German Legation was in charge of Romanian affairs. Since most of the Romanians were Transylvanians, they were served by the Austro-Hungarian consulates. The first Romanian minister to America was Dr. Constantin Angelescu, who was received by President Wilson on January 15, 1918. He was accompanied by Mr. N. Lahovary and Major Liviu Teuisanu. After his departure, Mr. Lahovary was in charge until Anton Bibescu arrived.

Mr. Bibescu, soon after his arrival in February, 1921, organized the diplomatic service and was very active in counteracting the adverse propaganda in America. He contacted many prominent Americans, lectured a number of times in New York City and organized Romanian exhibits here. He was followed by Mr. I. Cretzeanu who remained only a short while.

Mr. Carol Davila became Romanian minister to this country in 1927 and remained until 1938. He visited many of the cities in which Romanians resided, gave lectures, organized exhibits and gave receptions for prominent Americans. He remained in this country and was elected honorary president of the Romanian-American Alliance for Democracy and has written, lectured and campaigned for a more democratic regime in Romania.

Mr. Radu Irimescu, the former director of the Chrissoveloni Bank in New York City and Minister of the Air and Marine, became Romanian minister in 1938. One of his greatest contributions was to help organize Romania's participation in the New York World's Fair. After the present war began, he resigned as minister and became an American citizen. He is at present holding a responsible position with the Atlas Corporation.

During this time, there were a number of other Romanian commissions and delegations in New York. Mr. Serban Drutzu was named vice-consul in New York City in 1924. He was very much interested in the Romanians in America and has written two books on them in Romanian. He ceased to be vice-consul in 1929 and has since been employed as an engineer in New York.

Mr. Carol Tarcoanu, vice-consul in Philadelphia, was named consul in New York in 1930 and held this position until 1939, when Dr. Andrei Popovici became consul-general in New York. Dr. Popovici was among the most active Romanian consuls in this country. At one time, he was editor of "America," the Romanian daily newspaper in Cleveland, and has held other positions of prominence in Romanian-American life. He was a writer and lecturer, having also published a book on Bessarabia for his doctorate at Georgetown University, where he also taught for a short time. He tried to make Romania's participation at the New York World's Fair as effective as possible. He was instrumental in the founding of the "St. Dumitru" Church in New York City. At present he is associated with the American Banknote Company.

Queen Marie's Visit

Queen Marie's visit to this country will long be remembered by the Romanian group in New York. Her visit, more than that of any other Romanian, helped to cement the friendly relationship between the two countries. She arrived on October 18, 1926, accompanied by Prince Nicholas and Princess Ileana.

In New York City, she was given an official reception by Mayor Walker and Assistant Secretary of State J. Butler Wright. She travelled throughout the country and was acclaimed wherever she went. While in New York, receptions were held in her honor by the Chamber of Commerce, the Bankers Club, Columbia University, the YWCA, the Iron and Steel Institute, the Friends of Romania and a score of other organizations. She was given a warm ovation by New Yorkers on Fifth Avenue during her visit to the Public Library.

The complete account of her trip to America was published in a 238-page volume by Constance Lily Morris in 1927.

Romanian Participation at the New York World's Fair

There is no doubt that by far the greatest and most successful attempt to present the different aspects of Romania to the American public was the Romanian exhibition at the World's Fair. It was an impressive presentation of Romania's age-long past, her rapidly developing present and her far-reaching future. This was displayed in two buildings, the official building and the Romanian House, along with a separate tourist exhibit in the Marine Transportation Building. In the official pavillion, designed by Mr. G. Cantacuzine, and the Romanian House, built under the supervision of Mr. Octav Doicescu, Romania tried to present a picture of its national wealth. The technical bureau was in charge of Mr. August Schmiedegen and Mr. John W. Solomon was chief engineer. Besides the physical and material traits of Romania, it presented vivid glimpses of its intellectual and artistic life.

There were elaborate exhibits of costumes, varied in design and colorings; of rugs, patiently woven on hand looms; of wood carvings and of ceramics. Besides these, Romania showed what it had accomplished in the plastic, graphic and decorative arts and science. The methods of training its youth were portrayed as well as the reorganization of village life on a broader and higher basis.

The Romanian House presented a more intimate view of Romanian life. It was an expression of the spirit of the country. It housed a restaurant serving drinks and food prepared by famous chefs from Bucharest. It also housed the economic and historical exhibits. While dining, the visitor listened to Grigoras Dinicu's orchestra, to Fanica Luca's and George Stefanescu's Pipes of Pan and to the folk songs of Marie Tanase. On two occasions during the fair, George Enescu conducted the Philadelphia and New York Philharmonic Symphony Orchestras.

Following the closing of the Fair, most of the material was sent to Cleveland, where a Romanian Cultural Center will be built. Some of the material from the exhibits went to the Romanian Room of the University of Pittsburgh, and a part was presented to the "St. Dumitru" Church.

Many of the Romanians of New York were employed at the pavillion, and on different occasions, Romanian groups sponsored affairs there. On Romanian Day at the Fair, they paraded in costume and a group of them put on an exhibit of folk dances.

Spiritual Life

The Romanians of New York City are, for the most part, of the Eastern Orthodox faith. When they came to this country, they brought with them their faith which was and is a constant source of guidance and one of their greatest treasures. From the time of their arrival in New York some 40 years ago, their dream has always been to have their own church with proper facilities to house their cultural and social organizations. They were conscious of the fact that there should be in this great city a center representative of the culture of their native land. It was only recently, however, that their goal was finally achieved. Their scattered homes throughout Greater New York; the varied hours of employment; their association for the most part with people only from their own districts in Romania; and lack of a unified leadership were among some of the factors which retarded the realization of this dream.

Those who desired to worship in an Orthodox Church usually went to a Russian or Greek church; but on the whole, the spiritual life of the Romanians was neglected. Occasionally a Romanian priest traveling through New York held services in private homes. Old-timers recall services held by the following priests: John Podea, George

Branutiu, Octavian Muresan, Paul Craciun Sr., John Popescu and others. However, these services were few and far between and never reached all the members of the Romanian community in New York.

There were even attempts to establish a permanent church. The first was made by Rev. Epaminonda Lucaciu. He held services for the Greek Catholic Romanians in a chapel on West 21st Street from 1909 to 1912 every other Sunday, alternating with Trenton, New Jersey. After he left, services were discontinued and the Greek Catholic Romanians have- been going to the Greek Catholic Church in Trenton or to a Roman Catholic Church. At the end of World War I, Dr. Lazar Gherman rented a chapel on the Lower East Side and held Orthodox services there for nearly two years. There were other attempts, but they met with little success.

Finally, on September 30, 1928, a group of Romanians, including Dr. Gherman, Atanase Niculescu, Nicolae Ciuca, Ambrosie Neder, Theodore Leka, Phillip Leka, John Simo, Christy Baniot, George Dobosan, and Ivan Nicoloff met at the Casa Romana and founded the Descent of the Holy Ghost parish. Each member made an initial contribution of $10 and incorporated the church on December 6, 1928.

Nicholae Ciuca was ordained on their behalf and served this parish from February, 1930 to June, 1931, in a small chapel rented from the Russian Cathedral at 15 East Ninety-seventh Street. After Rev. Ciuca left, a petition was signed by the Romanian community asking Ambrosie Neder to become their spiritual leader. He accepted and was ordained by the Russian Bishop, John Kedrowsky, on July 15, 1931, and in 1935 was recognized by Bishop Policarp Morusca of the Romanian Orthodox Episcopate of America. He served the parish until June 30, 1940.

On a few occasions, services were held in that parish by Rev. Vasile Pascau and Rev. George Dobosan. The Descent of the Holy Ghost parish served the needs of some of the Romanians for over ten years and had many difficulties because of the depression; but they were not content until they could have their own church and cultural center.

In 1935, Bishop Policarp Morusca came from Romania to America and, upon learning of the plight of the Romanians in New York City, urged them to procure their own church, promising them his advice and help. Since the congregation of New York City was under the jurisdiction of Archpriest John Popovici, of Philadelphia, he sent letters in the early part of 1937 to the various Romanian organizations in this city urging them to meet and set forth a plan of work to obtain their own church. A meeting was called at which all the major organizations were represented. Mr. Louis N. Cipu was elected president of the committee of consolidation which was formed.

"St. Dumitru's" Church

At a meeting of this committee in August, 1937, it was suggested that the membership of the Descent of the Holy Ghost parish be included in the new framework and that they should work under its auspices; but because of the differences of opinion in this matter, not much progress was made. Therefore the greater part of the membership broke away completely and founded the "St. Dumitru" Romanian Orthodox Church in 1939.

In the spring of 1939, a committee consisting of Fredrich Palievici, Emilian Ovesia, Elie Florescu, Ilie Barbu, John Georgescu, Pandely Talabac, and Nicolae Chalamon was elected for the purpose of securing a desirable location for a church. Headquarters were temporarily established in the Imperial Hotel and immediately a special building fund was created to which Mr. John Georgescu was the first to donate $25. In due course of time, members and friends of this new parish made substantial donations together with the different organizations; "Dorul" Society donated $100; "Avran Iancu" Society, $250; "Farsarotul" Society, $500; the Sts. Constantin and Helen Ladies Auxiliary, $200; and the Sons of Romania, $25.

Dr. Andrei Popovici was consul general of Romania at the time and immediately gave his full support to this worthy cause, collecting many thousands of dollars for the achievement of the aim. Since it was out of the question to build a new church, a five-story building was bought for $14,000 at 50 West Eighty-ninth Street. Soon after the purchase, a temporary ikonostasis was built by George Z. Michaels, and the church was consecrated by Bishop Policarp Morusca in 1939.

The main floor was transformed into a beautiful chapel under which was built a spacious social hall, with kitchen facilities for serving up to 250 people. On the second floor may be found a reception room furnished in Romanian style, a library with over 1,000 of the latest Romanian books, a study, and the parochial offices. On the third and fourth floors are the priest's and caretaker's apartments. The plans for remodeling the building were drawn up by August Schmiedgan and John W. Solomon and construction was under the supervision of Mr. Emilian Ovesia. The interior decoration was put in the hands of Alexander Seceni, who built the ikonostasis, making it one of the most beautiful and authentic Romanian and Byzantine churches in America. The ikons were painted by Mr. Erimea, in Romania, and by Mr. Elie Cristo-Loveanu, of New York.

The Rev. Fr. John Trutza, of Cleveland, was called to help organize the parish. His wise counsel and guidance led to a speedy and sound church organization. The Rev. Fr. Vasile Pascau was finally named administrator and held services until a permanent priest could be elected.

In the Fall of 1940, Vasile Hategan, a graduate of Theology and the Faculty of Let-

ters and Philosophy in Romania was elected
to be the first permanent priest of the parish.
He was ordained on February 16, 1941 by
Archbishop Athenagoras and has since been
the spiritual leader of New York Romanians.

The church was formally consecrated on
October 25, 1941, by Archbishop Athenagoras. On this occasion, Romanians from all
nearby parishes attended the services and fes-
tivities of the day. Church services have
been held regularly on Sundays and holidays
ever since, and the church has been very active in an educational, cultural, social, musical and patriotic program.

Realizing that the future of the church
lies in the hands of the younger generation,
an intense religious educational program was
instituted, mainly through forums, discussion groups, mimeographed information, including a bibliography of all books in English on the Orthodox Church and the publication of a 176-page "Prayer Book for Eastern
Orthodox Christians," in which is to be
found a short history of the Church, prayers
for all needs, moral teachings, the Liturgy,
special service, and a catechism. The Romanian church has participated in Pan-Or-
thodox services and the ecumenical movement. Rev. Fr. Hategan has lectured before
numerous gatherings on subjects relating to
the Orthodox Church.

Through the medium of its library, the
Sunday School, and the "Nicolae Iorga"
Seminar, which it housed in its beginning
stages, the church has tried to make Romania, her church and her culture better
known. The Church Choir sings regularly in church and they have sponsored
events to make the Romanian music known.
On June 5, 1944, the church sponsored a
concert at the Carnegie Chamber of Music
which brought together a number of distinguished Romanian artists.

Besides having nearly 100 men in the Service, the church has always been alert to co-
operate with the wartime agencies. Its members have invested over $150,000 in War
Bonds and have made contributions of over
$1,500 to the Red Cross, the National War
Fund, USO and other worthy causes.

The "Cantul Romanesc" Choir

Soon after the St. Dumitru Church was
opened, the need for a choir arose. Mr. Nicholas Vamasescu, an accomplished choir director, formed the "Cantul Romanesc" Choir
in 1939, which has ever since given the
musical responses to the church services. Mr.
Vamasescu left New York in 1939, after
which Mrs. Rozeta Metes became director
of the group, which position she still holds.
Recently she has been assisted by Mrs. Cornelia Hategan.

Besides its church work, the choir has
given a number of concerts featuring Romanian secular and religious music. Many of the
male members have gone into the Armed
Forces, but the group has been able to continue its activities without interruption.

Sunday School

Almost every child in the parish attends
Sunday School, the age level varying from
four to eighteen years. It is a good omen
that they come regularly from great distances
to receive religious instruction. Instructions
are given in English and the prayers are
taught in Romanian. A definite course of
study has been planned for all classes. The
teachers are Misses Louise Babu, Polly Lupie,
and Xanthippe Costa. They are supervised
by Mrs. Cornelia Hategan. There are 45
children enrolled at present. Besides their
religious instruction, a social and recreation-
al program is provided for them.

Saints Constantin and Helen Ladies
Auxiliary

The largest organization in the church
is the Sts. Constantin and Helen Ladies
Auxiliary. It was founded for the purpose
of beautifying and taking care of the church.
Its purpose is "also to have its members, together with the president, help the church
at banquets and social events." All its activities and funds are under the control of
the church. It meets regularly every second
Sunday of the month.

The Ladies Auxiliary has donated many
hundreds of dollars to the American Red
Cross and to other patriotic causes. A group
of members have sewed bags for the Red
Cross to be used for holding gifts sent to veterans' hospitals.

Cultural Life

The Romanians of New York have very
many cultural manifestations to their credit.
There were organizations as well as individuals who have worked to make Romanian
culture known in America. New York City
has the oldest if not the only department of
Romanian Language and Literature at Columbia University, which was headed for
many years by Professor Leon Feraru and,
at present, by Professor Ilie Cristo-Loveanu.

Many books on Romania have been published in New York, and one of the greatest
collections of Romanian books to be found
outside of Romania is at the New York Public Library, the Columbia University Library,
the St. Dumitru Church Library, and the
libraries of the "Dorul," "Avram Iancu,"
"Farsarotul" and other societies.

Periodical Publications

At one time or another, there were at least
8 periodical publications pertaining to Romanian affairs published in New York City.
Most of them were published for only a short
time, but there were a few that came out
regularly for at least ten years. The first
Romanian newspaper to be published in
New York City, and one of the first in America, for that matter, was the "Ecoul Amer-
icii." first published in 1904. It was well
written, but unfortunately, it ceased publication after a few numbers. The "Romanul-

American" was a weekly newspaper edited by the Rev. Fr. Epaminonda Lucaciu, assisted by Victor Achim and Iancu Roman, from 1910 to 1912. It was circulated among all the Romanians in America and especially among those of the Greek-Catholic faith. When Rev. Lucaciu left New York, it ceased publication.

The newspaper that was published over the longest span of time in New York was the "Steaua Romana." It was published weekly by P. Axelrad from 1911 to 1924 and was primarily concerned with advertising Mr. Axelrad's Romanian bookstore. Among its editors were E. V. Ivanovici and Vasile Pop, who published it under better conditions for a year or so during World War I. In 1924, Prof. Leon Feraru cooperated in putting it out in magazine form with Romanian and English text, but it was discontinued shortly after that.

Iancu Roman published the "Desteapta-te Romane" from 1911 until shortly after the outbreak of World War I. In 1914, he also published the 'Calendarul Instrainatului." "Ecoul American" was published weekly beginning February 7, 1924, and later became a bi-monthly magazine. It was well written by a professional newspaperman from Romania, Lucian Marcu. It, like the others, had only a short existence.

The "Curierul-American" was published from 1923 to 1928. The largest number of shares in this enterprise were owned by Mr. Pandely Talabac. Mr. Louis N. Cipu also contributed substantially to its publication, together with members of the "Farsarotul" Society. Lucian Marcu was its first editor. At one time, the editors were the Rev. F. Octavian Muresan and Anthony Nichols. One page was published in the Macedo-Romanian dialect.

There were also two periodical publications on Romania, published in English. They were "Roumania," a quarterly magazine published by the Friends of Roumania Society and "The Roumanian Bulletin," edited by Basil Alexander. Details on these two publications will be found elsewhere in this article.

The Association of Romanian Students in America

After World War I, a number of Romanian students came to this country to study at American universities. At one time, there were enough in New York City to form the Association of Romanian Students in America. They collaborated with Prof. Leon Feraru, of Columbia University, in lecturing to Romanian-Americans and to other groups.

For over 35 years, New York City had the largest Romanian bookstore and publishing house, which was owned up to the time of his death in 1943, by P. Axelrad.

Friends of Romania

There is probably no other American cultural organization that has done more in the last 20 years to make Romania known to prominent Americans than the Friends of Romania Society. When one speaks of this organization, one immediately associates it with William N. Cromwell, one of the best American friends Romania has ever had. He has spent hundreds of thousands of dollars in promoting good will between these two countries.

The origin of the society goes back to World War I. At the time, Mr. Cromwell was very active in helping France and her allies. In this way he came to know Romania; and admiring the work of King Ferdinand and Queen Marie, he organized the Romanian Relief Committee of America for the purpose of collecting funds to help the Romanian wounded and destitute. His devotion to the cause endeared him to all Romanians.

One would expect that after the war, the committee would be dissolved, but in 1920, the Crown Prince Carol paid a visit to America; and at a dinner in Mr. Cromwell's home, thanked him personally for his work on behalf of Romania and her people. Being sincerely convinced that the new friendship between Romania and America should be strengthened even more, Cromwell organized the Friends of Romania Society on September 13, 1920, under the honorary presidency of the Crown Prince and the patronage of Queen Marie.

The purpose of the society as explained by Mr. Cromwell was to "perpetuate and develop the existing friendship between the peoples of the Kingdom of Romania and of the United States of America by promoting mutual knowledge and appreciation with regard to their respective histories, literature, art, language, conditions and achievements, and, generally, by the acquisition and dissemination of information concerning said countries."

The Society accorded an official welcome to this country to all prominent Romanian guests, including Romania's ministers to America, senators, deputies, industrialists and church dignitaries. It also published a number of pamphlets setting forth the economic and political position of Romania with a special reference to the United States. Among these were "The Romanian Question," "The Romanian Nation," and "The Romanian Kingdom," by Vasile Stoica; and "Bessarabia" by A. Bibescu.

During the period immediately following World War I, money was sent for the relief of Romanian children rendered destitute. With the society's help, the Romanian contribution to America was set forth at the exhibition called America's Making, which took place in New York in 1921. Under the society's auspices, Mrs. Margot Asquith delivered her last lecture in this country at the Waldorf-Astoria in 1922, bringing together the most eminent figures in the political, financial, and journalistic world of America.

The society published a quarterly magazine, "Roumania," which was the best magazine on Romania printed in English. The magazine developed from an earlier publication, "Statistics and Review of Developments," which originated at the time of the Titulescu Debt Commission. Mr. E. J. Sadler, a director of Standard Oil, gave the $1,000 which made possible the first issue's printing in October, 1929. Mr. Cromwell took up and continued its financing not covered by subscriptions and advertising. Among the many literary contributors were the late Herbert Adams Gibbons, Walter Littlefield, R. P. Wilson, Herbert L. Matthews, C. U. Clark, Max Winkler, Frank Stevens, Whit Burnett and a score of others.

The society maintained a permanent office and acted as an information bureau in aiding businessmen and corporations desiring to establish industrial relations with Romania. Mr. Horia Babes was secretary of the society for many years. At present, most of the archives are in the possession of the "St. Dumitru" Church, and activities have been discontinued temporarily because of the war.

Club of Romanian-American Citizens— Sons of Romania

The Club of Romanian-American Citizens was founded on September 28, 1924 by Messrs. N. S. Neamtz, Ilie Florescu, George Raducan, Nicolae Avram, William Stifter, Mihail Marginean, Theodor Figarovsky, Vasile Viorica, Vasile Jederan, George Muntean, Ambrosie Neder, John Raica, Pompei Todor, Alexandru Croitor and others. The purpose of the club was to promote a closer understanding of the American ideals and way of living, to make Romania known in this country and to foster Americanization of Romanians living here.

The club sponsored many events, but nevertheless, the group ceased to function and a new organization, The Sons of Romania, was formed. Basil Alexander was elected president and remained its most active member. He published a number of articles in the leading newspapers and some pamphlets combatting adverse propaganda on Romania.

The association organized a number of concerts, lectures and exhibits and brought together many Americans interested in Romania. Its annual May 10th affair was always outstanding. They were always ready to welcome prominent Romanians visiting America.

In May 1932, Mr. Alexander edited "The Romanian Bulletin" published in English to establish useful information on Romanian and Romanian-American life. The paper was well written and distributed free of charge for two years, after which it ceased publication. At present, The Sons of Romania is inactive. Its members have diverted their time and energy to the American war effort.

Nicolae Iorga Seminar

Probably the only seminar of Romanian language and literature in America is the "Nicolae Iorga" Seminar, founded on March 25, 1942, by Mrs. Eufrosina Dvoichenko-Marcov, a collaborator of the late Nicolae Iorga. Its courses were held at first in the social hall of the "St. Dumitru" Church and attracted many eminent professors and students of Romanian culture. It eventually became part of the French Free University and courses are held twice weekly on their premises. The seminar sponsored a commemoration of Professor Iorga, at which Professors Focillion, Gregoire, Halechi, Mirkin and other famous personalities spoke on Romania before a distinguished gathering. Mrs. Dvoichenko-Marcov, the founder, is also working for the War Department on an English-Romanian dictionary of military terms and is preparing a book on the influence of Jefferson on Eastern Europe in which Professor Schinard of Princeton, and the Guggenheim Foundation are interested.

Books on Romania

Most of the books and pamphlets in English on Romanian subjects in America have been published in New York City. A survey will reveal nearly fifty such publications, but we will note just a few of the most important.

Charles U. Clark, professor emeritus, who has travelled extensively and studied Romania, has written three books on Romania, giving a complete historical, literary, economic and social picture of its people. They are "Greater Romania" in 1922, "Bessarabia" in 1927 and "United Romania" in 1932. There is no doubt that one of the best histories on Romania in English is that published by R. W. Seton-Watson. The American edition was published in New York City in 1934.

A number of booklets and leaflets on Romania and especially on her physical beauties, have been put out by Steamship lines and companies with interests in Romania, such as "Romania Today," published by the Industries Publishing Company in 1928, and "Romania" published by the International Telephone and Telegraph Company. Hundreds of thousands of pamphlets on Romania and her people were distributed at the New York World's Fair.

A good general book on Romania was written by J. S. Roucek ("Contemporary Roumania and Her Problems," 1932) who was greatly helped by the Friends of Romania Society in New York.

Miss Juliet Thompson's "Old Romania" was one of the latest books on the subject to be published in New York City. It came out in 1939. (Copies may be procured from the author of this article). Besides a short historical survey of the country, Miss Thompson includes a number of full-page pictures taken by herself, with explanations. A book widely distributed among Romanian's in America was Titus Podea's "Transylvania," with Romanian and English texts. Mr. Podea is residing at present in New York City.

Other Romanians who are living or have lived in New York and have published books on Romania are Dr. Andrei Popovici, whose book on "The Political Status of Bessarabia" is very well documented; Serban Drutzu, who has published two books in Romania on the Romanians in America—one in 1922 in Chicago, and the other, in collaboration with Dr. Popovici in 1926 in Bucharest.

Miss Christine A. Galitzi, while a student of sociology at Columbia, made a study among the Romanians in America and wrote "A Study of the Assimilation Among Romanians in the United States."

Correspondents and writers who have travelled in Romania, have written accounts of their observations, such as Walter Starkie's "Raggle-Taggle" in 1933; Countess Waldeck's "Athenee Palace" and others. Some took a sympathetic view, while others took a critical one. Besides all the original works, there were a number of translations of Romanian works published in New York. Queen Marie published "The Story of My Life" in three volumes in New York; Mrs. Lucy Byng translated Romanian stories and Marcu Beza's "Rays of Memory"; Prof. Leon Feraru wrote some original stories and translated bits of Romanian literature.

The late P. Axelrad, owner of the largest Romanian bookstore in America for over thirty-five years, besides his "Complete Romanian-English Dictionary," "Elements of Romanian," and "Romanian Grammar with Exercises," reprinted many religious and popular literary books in Romanian. There were a score of others who have also written articles, pamphlets and books on Romania in New York City.

Individual Contributions to America

Besides the contributions of the Romanian organizations, a number of individuals worked hard to make the different aspects of Romanian culture known in America. There were and are probably more Romanian artists, musicians, singers, and professionals in New York than in any other city in the country.

Mr. Ilie Cristo-Loveanu, a graduate of Romania's Royal Academy of Fine Arts, has succeeded in building during the 23 years he has resided here, a brilliant reputation; and is considered among the foremost portrait artists of our time. He painted the portrait of Vice-president Charles Curtis which hangs in the Capitol, and those of Lt. Gen. William N. Haskell, William N. Cromwell, Thomas Hitchcock, Jr., John L. Lewis, Ernest Schelling and many others. He has held many personal exhibitions both here and abroad, and his work is to be found in all the museums of Romania as well as in many collections in America. In 1940, he was appointed professor of Painting at New York University; and two years later, Columbia University invited him to be professor of the Romanian language.

Mrs. Olga Cristo-Loveanu, his wife, is a graduate of the Royal Conservatory of Music and Dramatic Arts in Bucharest. A lyric-soprano, she gave her first concert in the old Aeolian Hall, singing exclusively from Romanian composers. Other recitals followed in Town Hall, Carnegie Hall and in other great concert halls in other cities. It is interesting to note that Mrs. Cristo-Loveanu is the first to bring the beautiful and exquisite Romanian folk songs to this country in concert form. She also sings operatic and classical works and has appeared with many great orchestras.

A short while ago, death took another distinguished Romanian painter, Jean Paleologue, who brought to this country a reputation acquired in Europe. Alexandru Popini also made a name for himself in the world of painting.

In September, 1921, two Romanian artists, Rubin and Kolnik, exhibited their paintings in New York under the patronage of Anton Bibescu, Romanian minister to the United States. George J. Zolnay, originally from Bucharest, was a famous sculptor who built many monuments in America.

New York boasts of many musicians who have made Romanian music known in America. Nicolae Olmazu, Sandu Albu, Jean V. Nestorescu and D. Cuclin are eminent violinists who have given concerts in the city, but who have since returned to Romania or have died. Cuclin was also professor of Violin at New York City College. Socrates Barozzi is a violinist of the New York Philharmonic. Theodor Bera is also with that group.

George Finch (Pantilie), born in Roebling, New Jersey, is a violinist with the New York Symphony under the direction of Leopold Stokowski. Cornelius Codolban and Nicholas Mathey have made Romanian folk music known in America. Mr. Codolban had his own program on NBC and has played at the Rainbow Grill, the Maisonette Russe of the Hotel St. Regis and is now in his fourth year at the Casino Russe. Mathey has an album of Romanian works on the market and plays regularly over the radio. He is now at the Russian Kretchma.

Aside from these violinists, we have an eminent pianist, Mr. Grigorie Alexandrescu (Franzell). After giving concerts in over 300 cities in Europe, he came to New York, where, besides giving concerts, he has headed many orchestras and appeared on the stage, on radio programs, and in television. At present he is playing at the Henry Hudson Hotel in New York and is in charge of music at the New York Athletic Club. He accompanied George Enesco in this country on several occasions.

George Stefanescu is one of the few masters of the Pipes of Pan (Naiu) in the world. After playing at the World's Fair for two years, he played in many cities and is now at the Romanian Village on Broadway.

In addition to the aforementioned artists, there are many Romanian singers in New York who have made names for themselves in the world of music. Stella Roman is in her third year at the Metropolitan Opera. Christine Carroll made a big sensation last year when she sang for the first time with that same company. Lizette Verea and Ronald Rim, after successes in Romania, appeared in feature roles in the "Merry Widow" and "Rosalinda" respectively. Gloria Benson (Banciu) sings regularly over the NBC network. Mr. M. Bulboaca has given personal concerts and is a leader of church choirs. Mr. J. Niculescu has given a number of concerts in America with Mrs. Niculescu accompanying him on the piano. Recently, Joseph Cristea, a renowned Romanian singer, has established himself in New York City.

Peter Neagoe has won fame as an author, publishing two novels, "Easter Sun" and "There is My Heart" and a volume of short stories, "Winning a Wife." These three books were recommended by the Book of the Month Club. He has also had a number of short stories published in leading magazines. All his works were translated into a number of foreign languages. His stories are being used in literature classes in several American universities for style. All his writings deal with the Romanian scene and Romanian characters in their surroundings.

Leon Feraru, professor of Romanian Literature and Language for many years at Columbia University, has published a number of works on Romania, including short stories and poems.

Leon Negruzzi, a direct descendant of Costache Negruzzi, originator of Romanian prose has published works in French. John Solomon is the author of many poems and owner of a number of patents.

During the past twenty years, Mme. Anisoara Stan has made Romanian folk arts and crafts known in this country. She is the owner of one of the largest private collections of Romanian folk art, and she has exhibited it in many of the large cities of America. She has lectured over the radio, at universities, and before prominent groups and given courses on folk art. She was consultant for the 1940 Yearbook Encyclopedia Britannica on Romanian folk dancing and led the Romanian dancers at the National Folk Festival held in 1941 at Madison Square Garden.

Mr. George Enescu; composer, conductor and violinist; has conducted the New York Philharmonic Orchestra on many occasions; and, more than any other Romanian has made Romanian music known to the world, especially through his "Romanian Rhapsody" which may be obtained on several recordings.

Alexandru Seceni; architect, painter, and interior decorator; has introduced the Romanian art of wood etching in America. Since his arrival here in 1924, he has sold his products to the largest stores in America. The trademark, "Seceni" is well known among those who appreciate fine objects of art. His wooden bowls, serving trays and other articles have been reproduced and are sold all over the country. Mr. Seceni was in charge of the interior decoration of the "St. Dumitru' church and made the icons for the Romanian Orthodox church in Dearborn, Michigan. He has also arranged a number of exhibits for the Consulate General, Romanian Legation and various organizations.

Benevolent Societies

The oldest and most active Romanian organizations in New York City are the benevolent societies. The "Dorul" and "Farsarotul" Societies date back to 1903 and are still in existence. For the most part, they worked independently of each other, but on numerous occasions they cooperated for worthy causes.

During World War I, most of the existing Romanian societies cooperated in a drive for the Romanian Red Cross. The "Dorul" Society, together with the "Avram Iancu," "Farsarotul" and "Unirea" Societies, donated an ambulance to the Red Cross. A standard for the sale of Liberty Bonds during the first World War was presented to the Romanian Societies. It is now in the custody of the "Dorul" Society.

All the Romanian organizations donated and worked together for the founding and building of the "St. Dumitru" Romanian Orthodox Church and cultural center. During the present war, they are cooperating on the War Bond Committee and in other patriotic and charitable undertakings. Some of the organizations have found common ground to work upon in the ranks of the Romanian-American Alliance for Democracy.

"Dorul" Society

The "Dorul" Society was organized on November 1, 1903, at a meeting held in Petru Glafirescu's restaurant. Among those present were Leopold Figarofsky, president; A. Ionescu, secretary; Stanislau Topolschi, treasurer, Vasile Ionescu, Enache Cosma, Tascu Niculescu, Carol Petrovici and Vasile Gheorghe. Having no name, the club was known simply as the "Romanian Club," after which they proposed to call it "Carmen Sylva," but it was finally decided to name the group "Societatea Romana Crestina Dorul." The club is an independent group, benevolent, philanthropic, social and cultural. It was chartered in the State of New York on May 11, 1904.

"Avram Iancu" Society

The "Avram Iancu" Society was founded on February 21, 1909 by Alexandru Bacila, who was also its first president; Ambrosie Neder, Vichente Bugariu, George Zamfir, Corneliu Trambitas, Ioan Voichita, Alexandru Mosoara, Teodor Morar, Ioan Stanciu and others. Its other officers were Remus Georgevici, vice-president, George Zamfir, recording secretary; George Flusiu, financial secretary; Vichente Bugariu, treasurer; Vasile Popovici and Stefan Borlea, auditors.

The society's standards were blessed on May 30, 1916. In a procession on Fifth Avenue, headed by 50 Romanian flags, they were taken to St. Patrick's Cathedral, where they were blessed by five Romanian Greek Catholic priests, led by Rev. Epaminonda Lucaciu.

During World War I, they contributed over $500 to the Red Cross, gave $200 toward buying an ambulance for the Army and also donated to the National Fund, toward a National Fleet, for the University at Valenii-de-Munte, and to the General Dragalina Lyceum in Romania.

On May 6, 1917, a committee of Romanian women under the direction of Mrs. Ambrosie Neder was formed under the auspices of the "Avram Iancu" Society to work with the Red Cross to collect clothing and shoes for Romania. They collected $2,418 and bought thirty crates of bandages, cotton and medical instruments which they sent to Romania.

After the war, the society sponsored various social events, the proceeds of which went to orphans in Romania. In 1927, they contributed $100 toward a fund to help cover expenses of the Romanian professors who were guests of Columbia University.

The society observed its 25th anniversary in 1932 with great pomp. Mr. Friderich Palievici was president at the time. When there was talk of building a church in New York City, they were ready to support the idea, donating $250 to the cause. Today, in its 37th year, the society meets regularly every first Saturday of the month in the social hall of the "St. Dumitru" Church.

The Avram Iancu Society is a member of the Union and League of Romanian Societies in America. Rev. Ambrosie Neder is the oldest member of the society; he was one of the founders.

The "Farsarotul" Society

The "Farsarotul" Society is the largest and most active Macedo-Romanian society in America. With the home office in New York City, it has a total active membership of 168, with branches in Bridgeport, Connecticut; Woonsocket, Rhode Island; North Grovenersdale, Connecticut; and St. Louis, Missouri. At one time, it had branches in San Francisco, Central Falls and other cities.

The society was founded on September 13, 1903, through the efforts and initiative of Nicolae Cican, who was among the first Macedo-Romanians to migrate to this country. He gave the society leadership through the first years of its organization.

It was first named the "Speranta" Society, but on December 10, 1906, the name was changed to the "Farsarotul" Society, because their forefathers were originally from Pharsala. Its members are called "farsarotsi,"

most of them having emigrated from Coritza, Pleasa and Disnitza, Albania. The society was incorporated on Dec. 22, 1909, in the State of New York.

It was founded primarily along patriotic and humanitarian lines, with the purpose of helping widows, orphans, and invalids, and building Romanian schools and churches in the villages from which the members came. In 1918, with a fund of $6,025, it was decided to pay a death benefit to the family of any member who died. The society has since paid out almost $10,000.

Among its many patriotic deeds and benefactions are the following: help rendered to widows, orphans and invalids, $5,000; donation for construction of a church in Coritza, Albania, $6,000; loan to that church, $2,000; donations toward remodeling schools in Coritza, Pleasa and Nevesca, $1,500; donations for construction of churches in Bridgeport, Woonsocket, Southbridge and New York City, $1,750; donation to church in Frasari, Romania, 50,000 lei; donations to those whose houses were burned in Frasari, 400,000 lei. These are only the most important benefactions, but there are numerous others.

The society has about 160 sons of its members and former members serving in the American Armed Forces, and has invested $4,070 in War Bonds, with a motion now pending for $2,000 more.

"Perivolea"

The "Perivolea" Society was founded on April 22, 1909, primarily through the efforts of Cristea Constantinescu, who was also its first president. It takes its name from the village of Perivolea, in Greece, from which all the members migrated. Perivolea is a village of about 2,000 inhabitants, all Romanian. They are a very patriotic group, deeply attached to their homeland. Many of them refused to go to Greek schools, and instead, attended the Romanian schools at Janina, Grebina or Salonika. A large number migrated to Romania proper, and a smaller number came to America, especially from 1909 to 1915. Very few left their homeland after the war.

Whereas their principal occupations in Greece were lumbering, sheep-raising and small businesses, most of them went into the restaurant business in America. Many of them went to Perivolea to marry, then returned to America.

The greatest number of Perivoleats are residing in New York City, about fifty families in all, comprising approximately 180 persons. There are also a number of them in Texas, especially in Dallas and Galveston; and some of them may be found in Albuquerque, St. Louis, Chicago, Minneapolis, St. Paul, Milwaukee and Detroit. In all there are about 100 families of them, or 400 individuals, in America.

The "Perivolea" Society is benevolent. A peculiar feature of the society is that it absolutely does not admit anyone to its membership who did not come from Perivolea. It does not meet regularly, but rather as the need arises, and its meetings are held in the social hall of the St. Dumitru Church.

The society formerly paid $250 death insurance, but that sum has lately been reduced to $150. A few years ago, it was voted that the wives of the members might also become members of the organization. The group has always given its full support to Romanian matters. They helped orphans, built public facilities and made other improvements in Perivolea. Mr. Eftimie Bey is president of the society, George Tegu-Iani, is the secretary, and Cocea Economu is treasurer.

The "Unirea" Society

The "Unirea" Society was founded on January 1, 1909, by Macedo-Romanians from the villages of Gramaticova, Candruva, Patecina, and Horupani, electing the following officers: George Popescu, president; Nicholas Dimaca, vice-president; Cocia D. Tasi, treasurer; Leon Zega, secretary; Laca Vangheli, auditors; Hirista Ionescu, Ghita Juja and Tolea Gumeni, councillors.

In 1912, a group of Macedo-Romanians from the same villages founded another society for identically the same purpose, in Indianapolis, naming it the "Picurar" Society. The "Unirea" Society immediately set out to merge these two groups and their aim was achieved on January 1, 1917, in Indianapolis. During the first World War, the society worked together with the other Romanian organizations in New York City to donate an ambulance to the Romanian Red Cross. Together with the "Farsarotul" and "Perivolea" societies, they fought for the liberty and independence of the Macedo-Romanians in the Balkan Peninsula.

In 1917, the society had over 400 members, being one of the largest Macedo-Romanian societies in America. After the war, many of the members returned to their former homes in Europe and founded branches of the society there. They sent a delegation to Romania, asking that they be colonized. Many of them were colonized in Caliacra (Dobrogea). Quite a few of the members transferred to the "Farsarotul" Society, and at present the "Unirea" Society is dormant.

"Vitolia" Society

Many of the members of the "Vitolia" Society, founded in April, 1944, are Macedo-Romanians. It gets its name from the town of Monastir (Bitolj) from which the members migrated. Even though it is a new organization, it has made amazing progress. It held its first annual entertainment and ball on December 2, 1944. It is a member of the Monastriotans Benevolent Brotherhood.

The "I. C. Frimu" Society

The Romanian section of the International Workers Organization is the largest worker's organization among Romanians in America,

with headquarters in New York City. It has societies in most of the cities in which Romanians reside, two of which are in New York City, the "I. C. Frimu" and "Romanian-American" Societies.

The "I. C. Frimu" Society, No. 4502 of the I. W. O. was founded in New York City in April, 1931, by the members of the Cultural Club of Romanian Workers in New York. In line with the program of the I. W. O., it worked toward a clarification and solution of the economic problems of the workers. On this basis, the society organized the Romanian Committee for Social Insurance, with the help of two other organizations in New York. They also helped organize the Committee for the Aid of the Victims of Terror in Romania.

The members of the society participated in the strikes for the benefit of the workers, it has helped to print and distribute literature for workers, it has supported the Workers' Press and especially the "Desteptarea" newspaper and has protested against the persecution of foreign-born workers.

When the Romanian-American Alliance for Democracy was formed, they were one of the first organizations to take part in the New York section. At present, Miss Sarah Popa is president of the society. Some of its members, such as George Vocila, George Pojar and Mrs. Margaret Pappas are very active in the ranks of the Romanian workers in America. In 1944, some of the members of the society formed the "Romanian-American" Society in the Bronx.

Political Clubs

The only attempt to organize the New York Romanians politically, was made by Dr. Julius I. Klepper, who organized the Romanian Democratic Club in 1936. The club has been active, mostly during political campaigns, and especially during presidential elections. The Republican Party usually maintained a Romanian section at its headquarters during campaigns. Romanians belong to both the Democratic and Republican parties and in all probability, also to some of the minor political groups.

The Romanian-American Alliance for Democracy

After the outbreak of the present war, the Romanians in America, desirous of doing their share in promoting the American war effort, organized the Romanian-American Alliance for Democracy. A call from the national organization to the different cities was sent out, and so it was that a meeting was called in the early part of 1942 in New York City.

The organization sent a number of telegrams to the President, reassuring him of the loyalty of the Romanians and sponsored public meetings to clarify matters in regard to the political situation in Romania. On

July 25, 1943, the New York Chapter of the Alliance presented an ambulance to the Army, together with the New Jersey Chapter. Mr. Nicholas Oprescu, by donating $150 toward the vehicle, was the sponsor.

Women's Organizations

The Romanian women of New York have founded organizations at a much later date than the men have. At present there is only one organization in New York of which the membership is composed exclusively of women. It is the Saints Constantin and Helen Auxiliary of the "St. Dumitru" Church. There were at one time two other women's organizations, the "St. Papadina" Society and the "Doamna Elena Cuza" Club.

The "St. Papadina" Ladies Aid

The "St. Papadina" Ladies Aid was founded on February 2, 1932, among the Macedo-Romanian women, principally through the efforts of Mrs. Sofia Cordista. The organization was dedicated to the memory of Romanian mothers. After the death of Mrs. Cordista in March, 1936, the organization ceased to function. When the S.S. Constantin and Helen Ladies Auxiliary was founded in 1937, Mr. Atanase Cordista turned the funds over to them with the understanding that an icon of the Purification of the Virgin Mary would be placed in the church. He augmented the fund with collections made in Bridgeport and New York, and the group gave a tea in November, 1944, to raise more funds. The icon, costing $100, was blessed on February 4, 1945, and formally given over to the church. The sponsors were Mrs. Paraschiva Kisilencu and Mrs. Maria Cipu.

The "Doamna Elena Cuza" Club

Since all the Romanian organizations were founded by men and primarily for men, a group of Romanian women founded the "Doamna Elena Cuza" Club in 1936, for social, cultural and philanthropic purposes. Among the founding members were Miss Mary Nedescu and Mesdames Catherine Nedescu, Elizabeth Vidican, C. Constantinescu and M. Stefanescu. They put themselves under the auspices of the International Center of the Y. W. C. A., where they also held their meetings. They have given many plays and arranged other affairs, so that Americans in general could appreciate our culture. They have helped to raise funds for the Red Cross and other worthy causes by giving teas and dances. The name of the club was changed to "Regina Maria" but it discontinued its activities at the outbreak of the present war.

Youth Organizations

Proportionately, there are fewer young Romanians in New York than in other cities. There are also a number of bachelors living in New York. Inter-marriage with other nationalities is higher in New York than in some of the cities because the young Romanian people do not have an occasion to know each other. Very few speak Romanian. The new generation coming up has a better chance to learn Romanian and to meet other Romanians, especially at the "St. Dumitru" Church, through the "Cantul Romanesc" Choir and the Church Sunday School. Several attempts have been made to organize the youth along cultural and social lines.

"Mihail Eminescu" Club

The "Mihail Eminescu" Club was founded in 1923 by a group of men interested in Romanian culture and incorporated on May 23, 1923. Its first president was Mr. D. Simionescu. The group was very active until 1926 when it became temporarily stagnant. New life was brought into it when a group of young Romanians took over the leadership, under the presidency of Miss Helen Neder. Soon it had 60 members. The club put on plays and sponsored many cultural affairs.

Its members formed a troup of Romanian dancers. In 1934, its activities were discontinued.

The Young Romanian Social Club

The Young Macedo-Romanians organized the Young Romanian Social Club under the auspices of the "Farsarotul" Society. They sponsored many social and cultural affairs. The club is inactive at the present as most of the members are in the Armed Forces.

The Young Romanians of New York

The organization, Young Romanians of New York, came into existence in February, 1940, as a cultural, social and athletic group under the auspices of the Church of "St. Dumitru." It sought to foster harmony and fraternity among young Romanians by promoting a better understanding of Romania through the study of her literature, history, and contributions to world culture and humanity. It provided an opportunity for wholesome recreation among the young people who comprised it.

THE ROMANIAN AMERICAN
1946

Mr. Charles V. Romcea, holder of a
Master's degree from Western Reserve
University, and former Director of
Student Activities in a Cleveland
High School, discusses the place of
the Romanian American in our multi-
ethnic society.

Source: The New Pioneer, vol. 4, no.
4, October 1946.

THE contributions made by the various ethnic, racial, religious, and socio-economic groups found in the United States forged the American culture that we now possess and enjoy. What America is today is due not to the contributions of the English, the French, the Negro, the Catholic, or the Jew alone, but, to the composite contribution of all these people. Every ethnic, racial, and religious group contributed to the stream of our history a wealth of concepts and ideas. Each has added another thread to the tapestry of the American civilization. But we still find, even in 1946, hurtful discrimination against some of the minority groups which compose our people.

Walt Whitman's everlasting phrase, "This is not a nation but a teaming of nations", was strengthened by Dr. Louis Wirth, Professor of Sociology at the University of Chicago, in a seminar lecture when he said, "America is a nation of minorities". What follows is a story of a late and bewildered pioneer — Romanian-American — who through his process of Americanization became a partner in a colossal enterprize.

For nearly one hundred years prior to 1914, some fifty million emigrants set sail from the continent of Europe for a new part of the world. The greater majority of these wandering souls landed at various points along the Atlantic sea-board. The forces which drove them hither were many and they are too well known to warrant repetition here. Among these fifty million we find a small trickle of Romanians, seeking along with others happiness in a virgin world untainted by chauvinism, war, and fear.

Their coming here was not by chance but by choice. They endured many hardships, both at sea and after they landed, but they were willing to make these sacrifices knowing that their children would enjoy the "blessings" which they had sought for themselves but which they could never obtain, and in order that their offspring would some day be an integral part of a new life . . .

As it happened, the North American continent at first was populated by western Europeans, dominated by the English who originally were superior numerically. Hence, our culture, our language, and our ideals became predominantly English. Later, with each influx of immigrants from Europe, newer cultures and folklore were intertwined and fused with the old and so our nation was altered somewhat, yet it continued to remain predominantly English.

Romania, the Roman sentinel of the East, also contributed to America. Infiltration of Romanians into the American population has been both small, when compared with such countries as England, France, Germany, and Italy, and rather late; nevertheless its contributions have been proportionate to its numerical strength. This article will not try to parade the contributions of the Romanian-American except, perhaps, incidentally in unfolding their story.

Like every other immigrant, the Romanian, from the moment he passed through Ellis Island with a bundle over his shoulders, was confronted with the problem of adjustment. He had to make adjustments from a rural to an urban community, from an agricultural to an industrial community. This process of adjustment and assimilation was not an easy task.

Most of the Romanian immigrants were tillers of the soil. Statistics are unavailable to the writer to show the percentage of those who came from the cities as compared to those who came from the villages, but it can be stated, without fear of contradiction, that most of the Romanian immigrants were peasants. Once here, they settled, not as might be expected on farms, but in the cities.

Of course, there was a motive for making their homes in the cities. The majority of the first immigrants were men, who came here with but one design, namely, to better their economic status in the motherland. Their purpose was, to put it in their own vernacular, "To make a thousand and the fare" and then return. Many of them did just this. Others, who were more farsighted, found this country to their liking and so decided to bring their families, to become naturalized, to take their places among those who came, like them, only centuries before, and to help design the American way of life.

Those who remained here were driven by an innate desire to perpetuate the memory of many things they had left behind in their native country. Consequently, they built churches, organized societies and clubs; they began to publish newspapers in their own language. Since their inception, these institutions have been sustained, as is this magazine, through the efforts of their members.

How long these institutions will last beyond the extinction of the first, or possibly the second generation of Americans of Romanian descent, presents quite a problem, especially to the leaders of these various organizations. With the loss of the old members there will be left but a memory to be compiled, written, referred to from time to time, and perhaps cherished by those who will identify themselves as Americans of Romanian extraction some generations hence.

Yet, it seems all this was destined to happen. From its earliest beginning America has sought to homogenize its immense mosaic of nationalities. All nations and all peoples have contributed, good or evil, to its growth. It cannot be said that any monopoly of good has been vested in any one people found today in our midst. Yet, some ultra-Americans tend to discriminate and to prevent the absorption of the foreign element into the American amalgam and thus they work against the very thing which has made the United States the greatest power as well as the most highly respected of nations.

But let us return to our vanishing pioneer. The Romanian element of our population is disintegrating. In another generation or two it will not be easily identifiable. It is easy to observe what is happening to the second generation already. These young men and women are forgetting the Romanian language; they are breaking their ethnic line of demarcation and are trespassing and marrying into groups other communities of a more heterogeneous type; they are joining organizations which are different and new to them,— all as a result of the American process of assimilation. Regretful as it may seem to some, this bewildered Romanian immigrant, often uncouth in speech and shabby in appearance, will in due time shed his pecularities, give up his folkways and all that set him apart from the other people and become totally assimilated. It cannot be otherwise.

It is sheer delusion to believe that the second generation of Americans of Romanian descent could be anything but Americans. They could no more become Romanians even if they could still speak the Romanian language, probably with an awful accent, than the old stock Americans could become British. It is natural for our first generation to remain Romanian, just as it was natural for those who reached the shores of America in 1607 to have remained British. A life time of learning cannot be destroyed overnight.

It is not inferred, and the writer does not profess to say or intend, that the Romanian group should ever conceal its ethnic or nationalistic customs and folkways. That would be wrong. Instead the group should use its ancestral heritage to promote unity in America and develop an appreciation for its ancestry. In so doing it would realize the dream of its earliest pioneers.

WHAT PRICE ROMANIAN CUSTOMS?
1948

Nicholas A. Bucur, a graduate of
John Carroll University of Cleveland, and of Western Reserve University Law School, debates the
value of old customs in the newly
adopted country, first generation
Romanian Americans vs. American
born Romanians.

Source: The New Pioneer, vol. 6,
nos. 1, 2, January-April 1948; vol.
6, nos. 3, 4, June-September 1948.

THIS WILL BE a difficult article to write, the essential reason being that the subject matter itself is delicate. The article is intended to provoke thought and discussion and certainly is not intended to cause anger or altercation in or by anyone.

Let's pose several questions. Perhaps that will be the easiest and least painful entrance into the issue.

1. What value have Old World customs, particularly those of Romania, in themselves?
2. Have Romanian customs shaped or helped to shape any phase of our American culture?
3. Should the older generations of Americans of Romanian descent encourage the preservation and adoption of these customs by the younger generations?
4. What are some of these customs?

These questions are offered merely as a lead into the article and will not be answered in any particular order. But, keeping them in mind will establish the underlying theme, which is, to examine the relations between the older generations of Americans of Romanian origin and Europe, and then, between the older and younger generations here in the United States.

Briefly, I have asked myself on many an occasion, "What interest should I have in Romania? Why should I care what goes on in Eu-

rope? I'm an American citizen, native born, and American educated."

Well, aside from any humanitarian, political, or anti-isolationistic factors, the important thing to remember is this single fact: all societies which have served a useful and good function in the world deserve to be preserved, for no other reason than that they fulfill an emotional need found in every man's heart. The reference here is to the need for beauty and to the satisfaction of this need.

If some things have been useful and good, and these are intellectual concepts, then these things can be considered, esthetically at least, to be beautiful. If they are beautiful, they are desirable.

Now, remembering these concepts, let us see how they apply to Romanian customs. It is obvious that if Romanian customs have been useful and good, and therefore beautiful, that as an individual I should be and will be, out of deference to my communally human need for beauty, interested in these customs. Being interested in the customs themselves, I then inquire, "What is their origin? What brought them about? What is their background? What are the people like who gave rise to these customs?"

That is the trend of thought I should have at this point and I hope such is your reaction.

The next step is to see some examples. It is futile to discuss abstract ideas on paper, unless concrete examples are given, in forms of appeal to the imagination, in the cloak of imagery, to clarify the points offered. In that way we can attempt to avoid mutual recriminations later and sidestep the possibility that both of us were agreeing to the same thing but erred in defining our positions.

Examples of Romanian culture and customs which will be discussed at length, subsequently, are: Romanian influences in music, in literature. in art, in government, in politics, and in historical traditions. Further, under the heading of customs, we shall discuss such charming manifestations of the Latin temperament as: greetings between friends, the kissing of the hands, and various other social expressions of everyday intercourse, as extrapolated from all walks and stations of life in Romania.

While we think of it, we'd better put another thought to you. It is this. By the demonstation of the various customs of the country, we intend to show that the kernel of the society involved should be preserved not only because of its positive effect in the world, but that it should be preserved as a unit, as something to be proud of, as something to promulgate and nourish. This thought is borne out by one of the author's favorite theories: evolution of government. But this evolution of government must be accepted only in this sense, that when a people base their modern society upon the foundations of many centuries of struggle and progress they should be allowed to express themselves as freely and naturally as a nation as they do as individuals and as separate components of an overall harmoniously functioning group.

So, in reading this article, when you are studiously perusing the quaint customs which will be depicted, try to visualize them as a part of an overall pattern of behavior, as a special brand of activity which belongs only to the people herein discussed.

In addition, the author admits that while the customs are uniquely Romanian, the same arguments can be applied to any minority or group which has offered something positive to the world. But the author does not exclude them and says rather "Certainly. Preserve them, too." Remember, we do not minimize their value, merely because we now emphasize Romania more in this discussion.

During the course of some travel the author had occasion to meet Romanians all through Central and South America and will offer some experiences along this line, also, as additive illustrations.

In this first installment which serves more as a preview and apologia for anticipated rebuttal, the author cannot say more at present other than: "In the next issue look for specific examples of the statements presented in this text."

The author invites comment from readers. Realizing that the field is wide open on this question the author is willing to entertain opinions of any and all who extend them. The issue, as stated previously, is delicate, and the author wants your view on just how much historical tradition, in the form of customs and culture, affects government and society, and just what value does Romanian culture, in particular, have in relation to the younger generations of Americans of Romanian origin.

Part II

In the last installment we discussed the questions: Do Old World customs, Romanian customs in particular, have any value? How do they apply to the young generation here in the United States, if at all?

We came to the conclusion, by a syllogistic process, that Romanian customs are useful and good, therefore desirable, and therefore worthy of preservation.

Now let's talk about a broader phase of this idea of customs. It seems to me that customs are the manifestations of the various cultures and civilizations which exist in the world. It also appears to me that there is a continual struggle in the world, due to the fears of the various cultures in the world concerning each other. We all fear and distrust what we do not know nor understand.

Let's expand this a bit. Persecution, which is an advance stage of struggle and decidedly one-sided, can take many forms. It can be total annihilation. It can be a partial stroke, a slow paralysis. It can effect subtle transmutations in the culture which is being attacked and these changes can be caused by force, a slow but insidiously firm pressure, by stealth, or by seduction.

The religious aspect of history presents striking examples of persecution. The Christians were persecuted, as a quick glance at a history book will show, for many centuries, taking the bloody heel of such tyrants as Nero, Caligula, and such non-Roman enemies as the Arab sultans of the tenth and eleventh centuries. The Jews suffered cultural as well as racial persecution at the hands of the Nazis of the last war. The Negroes still are suffering intensely, but probably not as violently, in the way of racial persecution.

In a sense then, persecution is the suppression of culture, and it takes its active form by the oppression of the customs which are characteristic of the culture.

This leads to the idea that freedom, in the democratic sense, should allow the individual to express himself as a person, or as a member of a group, in whatever customs he wishes to choose, as long as he does not tread upon someone else's toes. Naturally, there cannot be a conflict of higher rights, otherwise our purpose would be defeated. But a democracy should allow this freedom of expression.

Look about you. The emigrants of Europe settled in the United States with the resolve of becoming citizens of this country. Yet they congregate in their own nationalistic cliques, in the beginning, and retain many of their nationalistic customs, reminiscent of the "Old Country." Why do they do this? Because it is what they are used to doing.

In their own way they are attempting to combine the best features of both hemispheres. They are abstracting the happiness, from as many sources as they can, to which they are entitled as human beings.

Man clings to his background. He cannot help it. He does what he is used to doing. He prefers the familiar to the strange. These traits are what build up customs. Customs nourish security and banish the unknown, or fearful.

On the other hand, as pointed out earlier, this can be carried to an extreme by attempting to enforce one type of culture upon another, and then the conflict arises. Further examples of this culture struggle are: one of the fundamental principles of the Technocrats is to wipe out the Latin culture of the South American countries, and to superimpose "scientific" living upon the people. The Communists intend, according to Marxian rules, to overthrow "capitalistic" cultures and substitute their own. One could at this point question the definition of the author in regard to the word culture as many feel that culture necessarily means fine arts, sculpture, etc. This is not the author's usage. He is still using the word culture as the manifestation of customs, and inclusive of same.

Here in the United States there is often a conflict of culture in the very same family, particularly those families containing first generation children. The younger generation is oftentimes impatient with the habits, views, and customs of the older. This could be either the natural growth of adolescence, or a hypercritical attitude of the half-informed and half-matured, or it could actually be a clash of cultures. Take your pick.

The upshot of the discussion, then, is, in the eyes of the author, that customs are indicative of growth. Growth necessarily should be fostered, and in this type of life-situation, since the growth is gradual, the greatest care should be taken to allow the customs of each and every segment of being to grow. Progress is slow development. Let us not allow ourselves to be accused of impeding progress.

ROMANIAN HERITAGE IN THE UNITED STATES
1972

Prepared initially as a paper for the
1972 American Library Association Convention held in Chicago, this document
was improved and updated for the in-
clusion in this volume. Its author
is Vladimir Wertsman, who served as
chairman of the Core Committee on
Romanian American Materials within
the SRRT Task Force: Clearinghouse
for Reference and Acquisition Information on Minorities.

Library interest in Romanians living in the United
States started as early as 1922, when the Library Journal published a survey entitled "Romanians in the United
States and their Relation to Public Libraries" by
Josephine Gratiaa. It was a study initiated and sponsored by the ALA Committee on Work with Foreign Born.
No other survey has been published since in the library
press. Therefore, it seems useless to emphasize too
strongly why one feels the necessity to refresh our
knowledge on Romanian Americans and to review essential
information on this ethnic group. Otherwise, the re-
mark made by a Columbia University alumna in 1929 that
"Romanians in the United States are a picturesque, sturdy
group of newly made Americans of whom altogether too
little is known" would never be out of date.
    Our survey is concerned solely with Romanian Ameri-
cans and their American born descendants, by that, mean-
ing Romanian ethnic stock only. It is true that a
variety of other ethnic groups such as Hungarians, Germans, Jews, Ukrainians, Greeks, Armenians, etc., also
immigrated from Romania to this country. However, they
are beyond the scope of our study because in the United
States they have become part of their respective ethnic
groups.

Social and Language Background

Romanian mass immigration to the United States
started at the beginning of our century. Today, Romanian Americans form an ethnic group of about 200,000
people scattered all over the United States. Large con-
centrations of Romanian Americans can be found in New
York City, Philadelphia, Chicago, Cleveland, Detroit,
East Chicago (Indiana), Canton (Ohio) and Gary (Indiana).
    The immigrants grouped themselves in communities -

like other nationalities from the Old World - to share
with their fellows some of their common ancestral heritage, as well as new experiences on American land. Despite a strong trend of assimilation, many of their cere-
monies of marriage, baptism, funerals, their dances,
folksongs, costumes and even culinary art, continues today to possess a distinctive indigenous quality.

Romanian Americans are mostly of Eastern Orthodox
faith. The rest of them are Catholics and Baptists.
Their native language - to the extent that it is still
spoken - is Romanian, a Romance language, good cousin of
Italian, Spanish, and other languages of the same family.
However, it is an Americanized Romanian because it absorbed many English words, a phenomenon which reflects
the influence of the new environment, and the adaptation
to new conditions of living.

Unlike their ancestors who were mostly farmers, la-
borers and craftsmen, today more than 90% of Romanian
Americans are involved in factory work, small enterprises,
salesmanship, managerial and professional work.

Social Life: Organizations, Clubs, Associations

Organized Romanian American life began in 1902 when
the first mutual aid and cultural societies - Carpatina
(The Carpathian) and Vulturul (The Eagle) - were founded.
Soon afterwards, many other societies and clubs of similar nature came into existence, but some had only a very
short life because of bitter and futile internicine
fights.

An important role in the molding of Romanian American spiritual life was played by the Cultural Association for Americans of Romanian Descent which had an
existence of only eight years (1940-1948).

In our day, the strongest and oldest organization
is the Union and League of Romanian Societies of America.
It reunites more than 60 groups, clubs, fraternities,
etc., of different orientations, with a membership of
over 5,000. It promotes cultural activities, social
gatherings, conventions, and serves as a fraternal benefit insurance society, too. Then, there is the Iuliu
Maniu Foundation which helps Romanian immigrants with
resettling and integration problems and provides scholarships and grants to deserving students. It also organizes
cultural programs and keeps an interesting Romanian folk
art collection, as well as a small, but valuable, reference collection on Romanian heritage. Another organization providing assistance to Romanian immigrants and
awards scholarships to students, regardless of religious
beliefs or ethnic origin, is Romanian Welfare, Inc.

Besides lay organizations, there are religious organizations. From its very inception, the social life
of Romanian immigrants centered in great proportion

around the churches, because churches were not only places of prayer, but also community centers where immigrants
could get together socially and fraternally. In this
context, each religious denomination created its own organization. Thus, we have the Romanian Baptist Association of America, the Association of Romanian Catholics
of America, while the Romanian Orthodox Episcopate founded
the Orthodox Brotherhood, the Association of Romanian
Ladies Auxiliaries, and the American Romanian Orthodox
Youth. The main purpose of all enumerated organizations
is to promote the respective faith, although they are
involved in other activities, too.

Periodical Publications

The first Romanian newspaper in our country was
Tribuna (The Tribune), a daily published in Cleveland
(1903) for a very short time. The Romanian American
press proved to be very active and expressed a variety
of interests, political shades, national aspirations,
etc., ranging from the monarchist Glasul Romanesc (The
Romanian Voice) to the leftist (IWO - Romanian section
organ) Romanul American (The Romanian American). Em-
broiled in the same nature of futile disputes as the
different groups they represented, dozens and dozens of
periodicals have appeared and shortly afterwards dis-
appeared, leaving behind a long list of extinct publications.

Of the extinct publications, the most remarkable
was The New Pioneer (1942-1948) edited by Theodore
Andrica. It was the organ of the Cultural Association
for Americans of Romanian Descent, published quarterly
and entirely in English. It carried interesting articles
regarding the past of Romanian Americans, their contributions to this country, cultural events, book notes and
cooking notes. It is still a very good source of docu-
mentation and has been extensively used in our study.

At present, there are about half a dozen influential periodicals. A common characteristic of many
publications, reflecting the needs of the second generation Romanian Americans, is their switching from Romanian only to bilingual publications (Romanian and
English), with a tendency toward more English than Romanian (for instance, Unirea Almanac: 1972).

America (American Romanian News) is the oldest and
most prestigious newspaper. Founded in 1906, it is the
organ of the Union and League of Romanian Associations.
It appears bi-weekly in Romanian and English and carries
news pertaining to the Union, general news, and commentaries as well.

Three religious newspapers, Solia (The Herald),
Unirea (The Union) and Luminatorul (The Illuminator),
are monthly publications of the Romanian Orthodox

Episcopate of America, respectively the Romanian Catholic
and the Romanian Baptist associations. They mainly cover
religious news (in Romanian and English), but also contain general news, literary views, commentaries, etc.
   Following a long established tradition in Romanian
American life, America, Solia, and Unirea issue yearly
supplements called calendars which are, in fact, almanacs.
They contain, besides the usual calendric section of
holidays, numerous illustrations, poems, short stories
and organizational news. The religious almanacs also
contain directories of parishes and priests.
   Finally, there is Credinta (The Belief), a monthly,
put out by the Romanian Orthodox Missionary Archepiscopate in America, sponsored by the Romanian Government,
and Drum (Path), a private quarterly, cultivating literary
talents.

Romanian American Folk Art Collections

   Marilena Bocu and Anisoara Stan were the first Romanian American women to be nationally renowned as folk-
lorists and folk artists. They organized several exhibits
all over the United States in order to popularize Romanian folk costumes, pottery, paintings, rugs, table
linens, etc. Anisoara Stan also advocated the establish-
ing of a huge American ethnographic museum to house and
preserve the art and culture of all ethnic groups from
the United States. Even though her plan never came
through, she succeeded, at least, in conveying her message with respect to Romanian folk art. Thus, collections
of Romanian folk costumes, rugs and tapestry have been
preserved at the New York Metropolitan Museum, Brooklyn
Museum of New York, the Iuliu Maniu Foundation of New
York, and the Museum of St. Mary's Romanian Orthodox
Church of Cleveland, Ohio. The Museum of Modern Art of
New York displays interesting pieces of Romanian sculpture,
while Romanian folk paintings and architectural styles
as well as furniture can be viewed in the Romanian Room
of the Pittsburgh University.
   Among the private collectors of Romanian folk art,
one ought to mention Mrs. Dorothy Norris Harkness and
Dr. Donald C. Dunham.

Contributions to American Culture

   Despite their comparatively small number, Romanian
Americans have made interesting and important contributions to this country, and keep adding new threads to
the tapestry of American civilization.

Music

Being musically prone, like all those who belong to

the Latin family, Romanian Americans have displayed
numerous talents in the musical and artistic field.
Most distinguished among them were Stella Roman (cele-
brated New York Metropolitan Opera star), Lisette Verea
(comedienne, operetta singer and movie actress), and the
late Ionel Perlea (conductor at the New York Metropolitan
Opera, composer, and teacher at the Manhattan School of
Music). From the younger generation there is Marioara
Trifan, gifted pianist and holder of prizes from international competitions, and the Brothers Romanul who
appeared with the Boston Pops.

It is hard to say how many Americans know that
Benny Goodman's famous tune "And the Angels Sing" is in
fact a Romanian folk song brought by Romanian immigrants
and transposed into the medium of jazz. Then, the great
maestro himself - George Enesco - spent long periods of
time in the United States creating his well known "Romanian Rhapsodies " beloved, played and included in the
repertoires of all important American symphonic orchestras.

Movies

Jean Negulesco became a prominent movie personality
as a Warner Brothers film director. His innovative
spirit and talent were expressed in several dozens of
movies such as Singapore Woman, The Conspirators, Titanic,
Jessica, Three Coins in the Fountain, etc. Moviegoers
who saw the film Bathing Beauty heard Harry James and
his orchestra play the famed Romanian tune "Hora Staccato"
by Dinicu and Heifetz. Also, the melodious "Anniversary
Waltz" from the Jolson Story movie is a tune belonging
to a Romanian composer, I. V. Ivanovici.

Sculpture

Constantin Brancusi, considered by some critics
"the father of modern sculpture," won several admirers
and followers in the United States. Maiastra, Miss
Pogany, The Kiss, Bird in Space, The White Negress, etc.,
are well known and appreciated among many of his works
exhibited and acquired by the New York Museum of Modern
Art, Philadelphia Museum of Art, Art Institute of Chicago, etc.

Also prominent in the field of sculpture was George
Zolnay, as author of the Sequoyah statue in the United
States Capitol, the Edgar Allan Poe monument at the
University of Virginia (Charlottesville), the War
Memorial and sculpture of the Parthenon in Nashville, etc.

Painting and Architecture

Alexandru Seceni had painted icons and other

ecclesiastic adornments in several Romanian Orthodox
churches from the United States. He also introduced a
special type of wood etching highly appreciated in the
world of art, and designed the New York World's Fair
Romanian Pavilion in 1939.

Nicolae Ghica-Budesti designed the Romanian Classroom at the University of Pittsburgh, where one can find
fine examples of Romanian architecture, furniture, icons.
Elie Christo-Loveanu left a mark as a portrait artist
and painted, among others, President Dwight Eisenhower's
portrait at Columbia University.

Fiction

Peter Neagoe was the most talented and fecund Romanian American fiction writer in English. He published
several novels (Time to Keep, Easter Sun, There is My
Heart, et al.), abounding in simple peasant characters,
Romanian legends, folklore, and picturesque speech.

Eugene Teodorescu's Merry Midwife and Anisoara Stan's
They Crossed Mountains and Oceans added new reminiscences
about native places.

A very delightful sense of humor and wit were
brought by Mircea Vasliu, who revealed his writing
talents along with artistic gifts as illustrator in
seven books: The Pleasure is Mine, Which Way to the
Melting Pot, What's Happening, etc.

Poetry

John Solomon, Nicolae Novac, Vasile Posteuca and
S. G. Theodoru are noted names in Romanian American
poetry. Some Romanian American poems along with classic
and folk Romanian poetry were translated into English
by Eli Popa in his Romania is a Song: A Sample of Verse
in Translation.

Journalism

A central place was occupied by Theodore Andrica
who edited the prestigious Romanian American periodical
The New Pioneer (1942-1948), and served as Nationalities
Editor of the Cleveland Press for more than 20 years.
Important contributions were also made by Fr. Vasile
Hategan, author of several materials on Romanian heritage
in the United States. John Florea proved to be a star
photographer of Life magazine, while Ionel Iorgulescu
occupied the position of picture editor on the staff of
Redbook magazine, and concomitently served as designer
of sets for the New York Metropolitan Opera.

Medicine

Dr. Horia Ropshaw (physician), Dr. Anna Dumitru Poparad (anesthesiologist), Dr. Traian Leucutsia (radiologist), Dr. Valer Barbu (psychiatrist) are leading names and some of them served as university professors. But, the most outstanding in the field of medicine and biology is Dr. George Emil Palade, who was awarded the 1974 Nobel Prize - shared with two other scientists - for his contributions to the study and understanding of the cell structure.

Engineering

Constantin Barbulescu and Gheorghe de Botezat distinguished themselves in the field of aeronautics and ordnance; Dr. Ionel Gardescu was the first petroleum engineer to receive a doctoral degree from the University of California, while George Motoc made contributions in the field of metallurgy and chemistry.

Scholars

World famous are: Nicholas Georgescu-Roegen, Distinguished Professor of Economics at Vanderbilt University, who had a strong impact on American economists, and was described as "a scholar's scholar and economist's economist" by the Nobel Prize winner Samuel Samuelson; and Mircea Eliade, Distinguished Service Professor at Chicago University, a prominent historian of religion and mythology, and author of several books translated in many countries.

One can also add to the list of scholars Professor Sergiu Sergiescu (mathematics), Professor John Popa-Deleu (history), Professor Radu Florescu (history), Professor Paul Teodorescu (linguistics), Professor Nicolae Iliescu (linguistics), and several others.

Romanian American Research Collections

When Josephine Gratiaa published her survey mentioned in our introduction, Romanian Americans were a tiny ethnic group in formation, almost unknown in the United States. At that time, the major concern of public libraries was to provide Romanian books and newspapers for Romanian immigrants. Conducting a survey in that sense, Josephine Gratiaa arrived at the following conclusion: "Public libraries on the whole have done so far very little in the way of supplying books for them in their own language." A few years later, the situation was visibly improved because according to Christine Avghi Galizi, "...the public libraries of New York, Cleveland, Detroit, and Chicago have a fairly adequate collection

of Romanian books. The Cleveland Library has even made
an effort to attract the Romanians to make use of their
premises."

In the following years and decades, the above
mentioned libraries, as well as others - Brooklyn Public Library, Columbia University, Pittsburgh University,
etc. - have accumulated a wealth of Romanian books, and
English books about Romania, its history, people and
language, economic, social and political life, and many
other aspects. But in building their collections, some
of which are able to satisfy not only general needs, but
a wide variety of tastes and readers' levels, there was
almost no distinction made between a Romanian collection
in general, and a Romanian American collection regarding
an ethnic group. Romanian American materials are dis-
persed in different places, and no library, perhaps with
the exception of the Library of Congress, can claim
possession of a more or less complete collection on
Romanian Americans (history of their immigration, life
in the United States, contributions, newspapers, etc.,
in other words, any materials on Romanian Americans and
by Romanian Americans on this subject). As far as we
know, the Union and League of Romanian Societies of
America and the Romanian Orthodox Episcopate are the
best depositories of Romanian American materials. In
fact, they are also the best publishing houses for this
ethnic group. Valuable materials can also be found in
the Association of Romanian Catholics of America library,
and University of Minnesota Library, Immigrant Archives,
which serves as a research facility for the study of
American ethnic groups and immigrations from Eastern,
Central and Southern Europe.

Conclusions

As we are approaching the end of our survey, we
would like to accentuate that it is far from being a
complete study on Romanian Americans. It is only an
endeavor to draw attention to an original, interesting,
and creative ethnic group, which, for one reason or
another and maybe for no reason at all, seemed to be
forgotten for half a century by the library press. Our
study brought to light the necessity of an ample, comprehensive and general work on the subject, which would
have to start where Josephine Gratiaa left off, and
bring everything up to date. We still have a vast field
for research on the history of Romanian American periodicals, the development of Romanian American organizations,
the Romanian American language and its peculiarities,
and so on. And, of course, a major objective is to
build, or complete building, a good Romanian American
collection. It might sound like a dream, but I hope it
is not an impossible one.

ROMANIAN STUDIES ASSOCIATION OF AMERICA
1974

The Romanian Studies Association of
America (R.S.A.A.) was founded in
Chicago by several university professors from different American colleges
and universities. It is an expression
of the increasing interest in the Romanian language and literature in the United
States and Canada. The organization,
scope and future plans of the newly
created Association are shown in the
following material.

Source: Newspaper America: Romanian
American News. June 15, 1974.

Not too many people out-
side the academic world are
aware of the great, and still
steadily rising interest in
Romanian Language and Literature on the part of A-
merican and Canadian scholars, university and college
professors teaching at institutions of higher learning known the world over
for their fine quality of instruction. Such individuals,
in their great majority,
though they teach other
languages, step out of their
field of endeavor to devote
their time to research and
study of Romanian in its
undeniable Romance (Latin)
structure, exploring with
enthusiasm the untapped
sources of our national literature, exquisite art and
uniquely rich folklore, a-
mong other things.

Last year, in April, at a
Foreign Language Confer-
ence held at the University
of Kentucky at Lexington,
thousands of French, Italian,
Spanish, Portugese, German,
Scandinavian, Dutch lan-
guage professors held seminars in these particular do-
mains presenting scholarly
research papers and studies
on a variety of subjects. For
the first time, under the
guidance and sponsorship of
Professor Michael Impey,
now teaching at Princeton,
three Romanian sections
were added to the afore-
mentioned languages. At-
tended by professors pri-
marily interested in Romanian from the University of
California, Illinois, Washington, Chicago, Michigan,
Columbia, Stanford, North
Carolina, University of Utah,
Kansas, Portland State Ore-
gon, Princeton, Yale, Florida, Boston College, Mankato
State college, Minnesota,
etc., a diversity of topics
were discussed ranging from
linguistics to folk poetry,
novels and history. On this
occasion, Professor Vasile
B a r s a n of Mankato State
College read a 35 minute
study of the world-renowned
Romanian folk-ballad "Mi-
crita", Professor Norman
Fry of the University of
Florida analyzed **Liviu Re-
breanu's** novels, professor
Paul Vehlainen of Portland
State spoke on the subject
of **Romanian Folklore,** Pro-

fessor Charles Carlton of the University of Rochester on **Romanian Linguistics** (Comparative) etc.

The historic event of a permanent Romanian Studies Association of America occured last December during the Modern Language Association National Convention in Chicago. The MLA is the most prestigios organization of American university and college professors with a membership of 30,000 comprising English, French, Italian, Spanish, German, Portugese, Dutch, Scandinavian, Oriental, Russian, and now Romanian Seminars on Language and Literature. The Seminars are held annually either in New York or Chicago, in December.

At the 1973 National Convention of the Modern Language Association of America held in Chicago on December 27-29, 1973, the second seminar on Romanian Language and Literature was held, attended by university and college professors and scholars from various parts of the United States of America.

Chairing again was Professor Paul G. Teodorescu from the Monterey Institute of Foreign Studies (California), who opened the session with the most transcendental part of the meeting, the organization of the Romanian Studies Association of America (R.S.A.A.). As the creation of this association was decided at the first seminar in New York, during the interval between seminars all preparatory work had been done, and the draft of the Constitution drawn up and sent to many sustaining scholars and professors. Professor Norman Fry from the University of Florida presented the Constitution to those present who unanimously approved it.

Proposals then began from the different participants for the selection of the Executive Committee members. Although, according to the Constitution "the Executive Committee" shall normally consist of eight (8) persons," many of the nominees were not present and had not been consulted, a list of twelve persons was submitted for a vote.

These professors are, in alphabetical order:

Robert Austerlitz, Columbia University; Stefan Baciu, University of Hawaii; Vasile C. Barsan, Mankato State College; Charles M. Carlton, University of Rochester, Norman J. Fry, University of Florida; Eric Hamp, University of Chicago; Nicolae Iliescu, Harvard University; Alphonse Juilland, Stanford University; Kostas Kazakis, University of Chicago; Edward Neugaard, University of South Florida; Robert Rankin, University of Kansas; Paul G. Teodorescu, Monterey Institute of Foreign Studies.

The list was approved by vote from the floor.

The designated officers of the Association were also approved by a vote, and they are the following:

President, Professor Paul G. Teodorescu; Vice-President, Professor Charles M. Carlton; Secretary-Treasurer, Professor Norman J. Fry. NOTE: The secretary of the 1974 Seminar on Romanian Language and Literature is: Professor Vasile C. Barsan; 323 Floral Avenue; Mankato, Minnesota 56001 and is awaiting communications for the seminar.

At the end, the foundation of the R.S.A.A., the executive committee began the discussion of some business matters. Among these were the establishment of dues for membership, the delimitation of different types of membership, and the restraint of the annual bibliography of publication (Article 2, Paragraph 2c) of the constitution to only the area of North America. These amendments were approved by vote and have been introduced in the latest form of the constitution.

Since, according to the Constitution, the Association has among its purposes the publication of a professional journal, and the supporting of its members in publishing their works related to Romanian Studies, a special emphasis was given to:

a) The financing, e d i t i n g and publication of the **Yearbook of Romanian Studies,** a scholarly magazine of the R.S.A.A.

b) The publication of articles, notes, and book reviews concerning only Romanian Language and Literature in **Italica,** the official journal of the American Association of Teachers of Italian.

c) The publication of a volume dedicated to **Romania** in the series published by the "Review of National Literatures." (St. John's University).

It is understood that all interested persons publishing in **Italica** must have previously paid their membership dues to the American Association of Teachers of Italian. At the beginning of the Seminar, Professor Nicolae Iliescu briefed the attendants about his participation, as a representative of the Professors of Romanian, at the A.A.I.I. executive council meetings, about the agreements r e a c h e d on those occasions.

R.S.A.A. members interested in participating in the forthcoming volume **Romania** of the "Review of National Literatures" should contact the Special Editor of this volome:

Professor Nicolae Iliescu
Department of Romance Languages and Literatures,
Harvard University,
Cambridge, Massachusetts 02138.

In the second part of the Seminar, two presentations on Twentieth Century Literature were given by Professor Norman J. Fry and Professor Vasile C. Barsan. The excellent presentations prompted enlivening discussions and remarks.

Before closing it was unanimously accepted that the Seminar will be maintained for the next three years until it will become a permanent section at the MLA National Conventions. The following leaders of the Seminar were chosen:

1974, Professor Vasile C. Barsan; 1975, Professor Norman J. Fry; 1976, Professor Charles M. Carlton.

All the participants of the Seminar as well as the charter members of the R.S.A.A. enthusiastically committed themselves to the advancement of Romanian Studies on the American Continent and adjourned the session looking forward to the 1974 MLA Convention in New York. Dec. 1974.

**Prof. Paul G. Teodorescu,
Pres. R.S.A.A.**

BIBLIOGRAPHY

BIBLIOGRAPHY

PRIMARY SOURCES

Belknap, General William W. History of the Fifteenth
    Regiment, Iowa Veteran Volunteer Infantry. Keokuk,
    Iowa: R. B. Ogden & Son, 1887. An account of the
    regiment's participation in the Civil War, with
    documents stemming from General Pomutz, with his
    picture.

The War of the Rebellion: Official Records of the Union
    and Confederate Armies. Washington: G.P.P. 1886.
    A multivolume set in which one can find several
    pages reflecting acts of bravery comitted by George
    Pomutz, and the opinions of his superiors.

GENERAL BIBLIOGRAPHY

Brown, Francis and Roucek, Joseph. One America: The
    History, Contributions and Present Problems of Our
    Racial and National Minorities. New York: Prentice-
    Hall, Inc., 1952. Short background information on
    Romanian Americans.

Galitzi, Christine Avghi. A Study of Assimilation Among
    the Romanians in the United States. New York:
    Columbia University Press, 1929. Excellent basic
    book, with substantial coverage on the character and
    number of Romanian immigrants, their home background,
    distribution in the United States, religious and
    cultural life, organizations, press, old culture vs.
    new environment. Extensive bibliography.

Hutchinson, E. P. Immigrants and Their Children: 1850-
    1950. New York: John Wiley & Sons, Inc., 1956.
    Brings to light important social and economic as-
    pects of Romanian immigration in connection with
    and comparison to other ethnic groups. Based on
    the official 1950 U. S. Census data.

SPECIAL BIBLIOGRAPHY

Art and Music

Cross, Milton and Ewen, David. Milton Cross' Encyclopedia
    of the Great Composers and Their Music. New York:

Doubleday and Co., Inc., 1962. Volume I has a
chapter on George Enesco's life and music.

Jianou, Ionel. Brancusi. New York: Tudor Publishing
Co., 1963. Good biography accompanied by excellent
illustrations and fine bibliography.

Cooking

Stan, Anisoara. The Romanian Cooking. New York: The
Citadel Press, 1969. Intriguing and flavorful
recipes for 450 Romanian popular dishes.

Fiction

Neagoe, Peter. Easter Sun. New York: Coward-McCann,
Inc., 1934. Description of everyday Romanian
peasant life, legends, folklore, speech.

_____. There is My Heart. New York: Coward-McCann,
Inc., 1936. A Romanian peasant who starts out for
America, but before leaving gets involved in a love
affair.

_____. Time to Keep. New York: Coward-McCann, Inc.,
1949. Reminiscences of the author's boyhood spent
in a village in Transylvania with tender feelings
for the people of the countryside, of whom many
later became Americans.

Stan, Anisoara. They Crossed Mountains and Oceans.
New York: The William-Frederick Press, 1947.
The author's experiences as a new immigrant in
our country; several pages devoted to Romanian
folklore, customs, costumes, holidays, etc.

Teodorescu, Eugene C. Merry Midwife. New York: Hughton
Miffin Co., 1947. Memories about native places.
Relaxing book, but some expressions may sound
strange to Americans.

Vasiliu, Mircea. Which Way to the Melting Pot. New
York: Doubleday & Co., Inc., 1963. The author,
a newly arrived immigrant, struggles to learn English and to adapt himself to American customs.
Delightful sense of humor and wit.

Organizations

Fisk, Margaret, et al., ed. Encyclopedia of Associations.
Detroit, Mich.: Gale Research Co., 1972. Lists
Romanian American organizations and their specific
activities.

Periodicals

Wynar, Lubomir. <u>Encyclopedic Directory of Ethnic News-
    papers and Periodicals in the United States</u>. Little-
    ton, Colo.: Libraries Unlimited, Inc., 1972.
    Annotates the most important Romanian American
    periodicals.

Poetry

Popa, Eli. <u>Romania is a Song</u>: <u>A Sample of Verse in
    Translation</u>. Detroit, Mich.: America Publishing
    Co., 1967. Presents many facets of Romanian poetry,
    classic as well as Romanian American poets. Short
    biographies of translated poets are included.

Radio Stations

American Council for Nationalities Service. <u>Foreign
    Language Radio Stations in the U.S.A</u>. New York:
    1970. Lists all radio stations broadcasting Ro-
    manian language programs.

Religion

Mead, Frank S., ed. <u>Handbook of Denominations in the
    United States</u>. Nashville, Tenn.: Abingdon Press,
    1970. Describes the organizational structure of
    Romanian Orthodox and Catholic churches.

Romanian Language and Linguistics Study

Cristo-Loveanu, Elie. <u>Romanian Language</u>. New York:
    1962. Published by the author himself, the book is
    considered one of the best, most complete, and com-
    prehensive manual. Introduction by noted linguist
    Mario Pei from Columbia University.

Murell, M. <u>Teach Yourself Romanian</u>. New York: David
    McKay Co., Inc., 1972. Good for beginners.

Pei, Mario. <u>The World's Chief Languages</u>. New York:
    S. F. Vanni, 1946. Sheds light on the linguistic
    structure of the Romanian language, and its place
    in the family of Romance languages.

Schonkron, Marcel. <u>Romanian-English and English-Romanian
    Dictionary</u>. New York: Ungar, Frederick, Publishing
    Co., Inc., 1967. Contains about 40,000 words, in-
    cluding important coloquial and technical terms,
    and useful idioms.

PERIODICAL LITERATURE

Anagnastosache, George. "Romanians in America," The
    New Pioneer, vol. 2, no. 3 (July 1944), pp. 12-13.

Borza Jr., John. "Two Romanians in the Civil War," The
    New Pioneer, vol. I, no. 2 (February 1943) pp. 5-7.

Gratiaa, Josephine. "Romanians in the United States and
    Their Relation to Public Libraries," The Library
    Journal (May 1, 1922), pp. 400-404.

Hategan, Vasile. "Romanians in New York," The New
    Pioneer, vol. 3, no. 2 (April 1945), pp. 28-50.

PHONOGRAPHIC RECORDS

Bach, J. S. Concerto for Two Violins and Orchestra in
    D. Minor. Yehudi Menuhin and George Enesco,
    violinists, with Symphony Orchestra. Victor,
    Albums nos. 7732 and 7733.

Dinicu, G. Ciocirlia and Dinicu Melodies. Played by
    Grigore Dinicu Gypsy Orchestra. Victor, Album no.
    V-19024.

Dinicu-Heifetz. Hora Staccato. Played by Jascha Heifetz,
    violinist. Victor, Album no. 1864-A.

Enesco, G. Romanian Rhapsody No. 1 in A. Major (Op. 11).
    Performed by the Philadelphia Symphonic Orchestra,
    Eugene Ormandy, conductor. Victor, Album no. DM-
    830.

_____. Romanian Rhapsody No. 2 in D. Major (Op. 11).
    Performed by the National Symphony Orchestra, Hans
    Kindler, conductor. Victor, Album no. DM-830.

Hatiegan, John. Romanian Popular Melodies from Indiana
    Harbor and Chicago. Played by John Hatiegan and
    his orchestra. Columbia, Albums nos. 31042F and
    31049F; Victor, no. V-19020.

Stefanescu, George. Pipes of Pan, Romanian Shepherd
    Pipe Solos. Decca Album no. A-119.

Union and League of Romanian Societies of America.
    Romanian Songs and Dances. Presented by the Roman-
    ian Artistic Cultural Group "Sezatearea" of Cleve-
    land, Ohio.

APPENDIX

ROMANIAN AMERICAN COMMUNITIES

The communities are arranged in alphabetical order by state, and the numbers that follow after each community have the following meanings:
1. Union and League of Romanian Societies of America affiliations
2. Romanian Orthodox churches
3. Romanian Catholic churches
4. Romanian Baptist churches

ARIZONA:
  Phoenix, 1

CALIFORNIA:
  La Canda, 1
  Los Angeles, 1,2
  San Francisco, 2
  Sunny Vale, 1

DISTRICT OF COLUMBIA:
  Washington, 2

CONNECTICUT:
  Bridgeport, 1,2

FLORIDA:
  Hollywood, 1
  Miami, 2

ILLINOIS:
  Aurora, 3,4
  Chicago, 1,2,4

INDIANA:
  East Chicago, 1,3
  Fort Wayne, 1,2
  Garret, 1
  Gary, 1,2,4
  Indiana Harbor
  Indianapolis, 1,2,4
  Terre Haute, 1,2

MICHIGAN:
  Ann Arbor,
  Dearborn, 1,2,3
  Detroit, 1,2,3,4
  Grass Lake, 2
  Highland Park, 2,4
  Pontiac, 1
  Southfield, 1
  Sterling Heights, 1

Warren, 1

MINNESOTA:
  St. Paul, 2
  South St. Paul, 1

MISSOURI:
  St. Joseph, 1
  St. Louis, 1,2

NEBRASKA:
  Omaha, 1

NEW JERSEY:
  Roebling, 1,3
  Trenton, 3

NEW YORK:
  Buffalo, 1
  New York City, 1,2

OHIO:
  Akron, 1,2,4
  Alliance, 1,3
  Canton, 1,2,3
  Cleveland, 1,2,3,4
  Cincinatti, 1
  Hubbard, 1
  Lorain, 1,3
  Martins Ferry, 2
  Massillon, 1
  McDonald, 1
  Newark, 1
  New Philadelphia, 1
  Niles, 1,2
  Salem, 1,2
  Toledo, 1
  Warren, 1,2,4
  Youngstown, 1,2,3

PENNSYLVANIA:
  Aliquipa, 1
  Bethlehem, 1
  Ellwood, 1,2
  Erie, 1,2,3,4
  Farrel, 2,3
  Harrisburg, 4
  McKeesport, 3
  New Castle, 1
  Philadelphia, 2,4
  Sharon, 1
  West Homestead, 1

RHODE ISLAND:
  Woonsocket, 2

WEST VIRGINIA:
  Weirton, 1

WISCONSIN
  Milwaukee, 1

ROMANIAN CANADIAN COMMUNITIES

MANITOBA:
  Blue Wing, 2
  Lennard, 2
  Shell Valley, 2
  Winnipeg, 2

QUEBEC:
  Montreal, 1

ONTARIO:
  Hamilton, 1
  Kitchener, 2
  Toronto, 2
  Windsor, 1

SASKATCHEWAN:
  Assinboia, 2

ROMANIAN AMERICAN INSTITUTIONS & ORGANIZATIONS

AMERICAN ROMANIAN ORTHODOX YOUTH (AROY)
2522 Grey Tower Road, R.F.D. #7
Jackson, Michigan 49201

ASSOCIATION OF ROMANIAN AMERICAN ORTHODOX LADIES (ARFORA)
2522 Grey Tower Road, R.F.D. #7
Jackson, Michigan 49201

ASSOCIATION OF ROMANIAN CATHOLICS OF AMERICA (ARCA)
4309 Olcott Avenue
East Chicago, Indiana 46312

IULIU MANIU AMERICAN ROMANIAN RELIEF FOUNDATION
55 West 42nd Street
New York, New York 10036

NATIONAL COMMITTEE FOR REFUGEES
St. Dumitru's Church
50 West 89 Street
New York, New York

THE ORTHODOX BROTHERHOOD
11341 Woodward Avenue
Detroit, Michigan 48202

THE ROLLING ROMANIANS
(Wheelchair Track Team)
1448 West River Park Drive
Inkster, Michigan 48141

ROMANIAN BAPTIST ASSOCIATION OF THE UNITED STATES
7009 Detroit Avenue
Cleveland, Ohio 44120

THE ROMANIAN CATHOLIC RELIEF COMMITTEE
St. George's Church
720 Rural Street
Aurora, Illinois 60505

ROMANIAN NATIONAL COMMITTEE
78-14 32nd Avenue
East Elmhurst, New York 11370

THE ROMANIAN ORTHODOX EPISCOPATE OF AMERICA
2522 Grey Tower Road, R.F.D. #7
Jackson, Michigan 49201

ROMANIAN ORTHODOX MISSIONARY ARCHEPISCOPATE IN AMERICA
     19959 Riopelle Street
     Detroit, Michigan 48203

ROMANIAN STUDIES ASSOCIATION OF AMERICA
     c/o Professor Paul G. Teodorescu
     Monterey Institute of Foreign Studies
     Monterey, California 93940

ROMANIAN WELFARE, INC.
     93 Groton Street
     Forest Hills, New York 11375

UNION AND LEAGUE OF ROMANIAN SOCIETIES OF AMERICA
     1106 Williamson Building
     215 Euclid Avenue
     Cleveland, Ohio 44114

          ROMANIAN ART COLLECTIONS IN NEW YORK CITY

BROOKLYN MUSEUM
     Eastern Parkway & Washington Avenue

METROPOLITAN MUSEUM OF ART
     Fifth Avenue, 80th to 84th Streets

MUSEUM OF MODERN ART
     11 West 53rd Street

ROMANIAN FOLK ART COLLECTION
     c/o Iuliu Maniu Foundation
     55 West 42nd Street

ROMANIAN LANGUAGE IN AMERICAN UNIVERSITIES

The following American colleges and universities offer
courses in Romanian or have sections for studying the
Romanian language and linguistics.

BOSTON UNIVERSITY
    Boston, Massachusetts 02215

COLUMBIA UNIVERSITY
    New York, New York 10027

HARVARD UNIVERSITY
    Cambridge, Massachusetts 02138

INDIANA UNIVERSITY
    Bloomington, Indiana 47401

MANKATO STATE COLLEGE
    Mankato, Minnesota 56001

MONTEREY INSTITUTE OF FOREIGN STUDIES
    Monterey, California 93940

UNIVERSITY OF CHICAGO
    Chicago, Illinois 60637

UNIVERSITY OF FLORIDA
    Gainsville, Florida 32601

UNIVERSITY OF HAWAII
    Honolulu, Hawaii 96822

UNIVERSITY OF ILLINOIS
    Urbana, Illinois 61801

UNIVERSITY OF MICHIGAN
    Ann Arbor, Michigan 48104

UNIVERSITY OF NORTH CAROLINA
    Chapel Hill, North Carolina 27514

UNIVERSITY OF RHODE ISLAND
    Kingston, Rhode Island 02881

UNIVERSITY OF ROCHESTER
    Rochester, New York 14627

UNIVERSITY OF SOUTH FLORIDA
    Tampa, Florida 33620

THE ROMANIAN ALPHABET AND ITS ENGLISH PRONUNCIATION

A,a - like Art

Ă,ă - like bacOn

Â,â - like rhYthm

B,b - like Book

C,c - like Cook

C,c - before e,i becomes
       CH like Chess, Chill

D,d - like Dog

E,e - like mEt and some-
       times like Yes

F,f - like Fog

G,g - like Go

G,g - before e,i becomes
       GE, GI like Gentle,
       Gin

G,g - before HE, HI
       becomes GHE, GHI
       like Gebbie, McGill

I,i - like machIne

Î,î - pronounced like Â,â

J,j - like pleaSure

K,k - appear only in
       foreign words and
       are pronounced like
       killo

L,l - like Lemon

M,m - like Mother

N,n - like Noon

O,o - like Or

P,p - like Poor

Q,q - appear only in
       foreign words and
       are pronounced like
       in Quart

R,r - like Red

S,s - like Sort

Ş,ş - is SH like Shy

T,t - like Train

Ţ,ţ - is TS like hearTS

U,u - like moon

V,v - like Visit

W,w - appear only in
       foreign words and
       are pronounced
       either like W in
       the German WORT or
       like W in the Eng-
       lish WATT

X,x - like example

Y,y - appear only in
       foreign words
       like Yard

Z,z - like Zebra

The Romanian alphabetic notation is very close to the English one since both are using the Latin alphabet, the only exceptions being Ă,Â,Î,Ş,Ţ, which are specific Romanian additional symbols.

The Romanian language does not have definite rules of accentuation; the accent falls generally on the last syllable, as well as on the second from the last or even the third from the last syllable.

ROMANIAN PROVERBS & SAYINGS
(free translation and adaptation)

BOOK   A good book can take the place of a friend,
             but a friend cannot take the place of a
             good book.

BAD   Bad things should be written on running
             water.

CHILD   Whether the homes are big or small, a child
             is a blessing to all.

DRUNKENNESS Drunkenness is like an open door through
             which other vices keep coming.

EXAMPLE   The cheapest article is advice; the most
             valuable is a good example.

ENEMY   Better be a loser to a wise enemy rather
             than a winner over a foolish friend.

FRIEND   Do not leave an old good friend of yours in
             order to please a new one.

GOD   Those who keep the word GOD too much in
             their mouths, make space for the DEVIL in
             their hearts.

HEAD   Woe to your feet if you do not guide them
             with your head.

HOME   One thing, for sure, each couple can tell,
             one's home is both paradise and hell.

IDLENESS   Idleness is the biggest enemy of good luck.

JUSTICE   Justice always looks like the rulers make
             it look.

KNOW   The more we know, the more we realize how
             much we do not know.

KNOWLEDGE   Knowledge is like a tower in which you test
             and build your power.

MIDWIVES   Too many midwives at the mother's bed -
             The chatter is alive, but the baby is dead.

MODESTY   Modesty is the dearest jewel of a man's soul.

OXEN   While oxen are tied by their horns, men

are tied by their words.

SPARROW   Do not give up the sparrow from your hand
                 for a parrot on the fence.

TALK   Where there is too much talk, the deeds are
                 very poor.

THOUGHTS   Good thoughts are one's best pillow for
                 sleeping.

WIFE   A house without a wife is like a fiddle
                 without strings.

WINE   Enjoy drinking the wine, but do not become
                 drunk by it.

WISDOM   The roots of wisdom are bitter, but its
                 fruits are sweet.

WOLF   A wolf may change his hair, but not his
                 habits.

WORDS   Words are always cheaper than deeds.

WORK   A saying by grandfathers often told -
                 Work is wealth, it is like a bracelet of
                 gold.

ROMANIAN COOKING

Romanian Americans love good food, and like to prepare it in the tradition brought from their native land. Their food is both rich and varied, and is a mixture of Roman, Greek, Slavic, Hungarian, Turkish, Gypsy, German and French influences.

Romanian cooking is savory, not greasy, very flavorful, and stimulating to the appetite. Herbs and vegetables are used in abundance. One meal dishes occupy a central place in the index of recipes, but these dishes are very nourishing, cost little, and are easy to prepare. Even if sometimes the recipes are somehow complicated, Romanian women like to cook; they put their hearts into cooking, try to be original, and become veritable artists of the kitchen.

In continuation, we are going to acquaint the reader with some typical Romanian dishes and their recipes.

MAMALIGA (CORN MUSH)

This is considered a national dish, easy to prepare, digestible, and served in several ways as a substitute for bread.

Bring one quart of water to a vigorous boil, then sprinkle in slowly two handfuls of cornmeal, stirring constantly with a wooden spoon, and cook until the mush becomes thick and smooth. Let stand on a low fire about 15 minutes longer, or until thick enough to retain the shape of the pot. With the wooden spoon first dipped in cold water, press the mamaliga away from the sides of the pot, then turn it into a wooden platter, plank or breadboard.

Another variety of mamaliga is mamaliga au gratin, which can be made by mixing the mamaliga with butter and a generous amount of cheese. Then, spread in a buttered earthenware or glass casserole, cover with a layer of cheese, dot with butter and bake.

CIORBA (SOUR SOUP)

Ciorba is a very popular dish which is actually a soup seasoned with sauerkraut or pickled cucumber juice.

Ciorba with meat balls

    2 quarts sauerkraut juice
    3 large onions
    2 carrots

1 parsnip
1 parsley root
1 pound ground beef and pork mixed
1 egg
1 tablespoon rice

Boil onions, parsnip, parsley and carrots in sauerkraut juice and one pint of water. To the ground meat
add a little salt and pepper to taste, 1 egg, 1 tablespoon rice and mix well. Form round meatballs about
the size of a walnut and drop into boiling juice. Boil
until meat is tender. Remove vegetables and serve.

SARMALE (STUFFED CABBAGE)

Place 1 large fresh head of cabbage into boiling
water and let stand until softened. Remove leaves
separately, cutting off part of the thick stem end.

Mix: 2 lbs. pork shoulder, ground medium
      1/4 cup rice
      1 tbsp. salt
      1/8 tsp. black pepper
      1 medium onion chopped fine

Place 2 tablespoons of this mixture in each cabbage
leaf. Fold lower end over and roll. Tuck in top. Cover
bottom of kettle with a layer of sauerkraut and arrange
cabbage rolls on it. Cover with the rest of the kraut
juice. Add enough water to come up to the level of the
rolls. One can use either canned or fresh kraut. Cook
for about two hours.

GHIVECI (VEGETABLE STEW)

1 bunch carrots	1 summer or winter squash
3 large potatoes	1 cup stringbeans
6 tomatoes	1 cup fresh peas
1 green pepper	1 medium cabbage
2-3 large onions	1 medium cauliflower
2-3 celery roots	1/2-3/4 cup oil (olive or
1-2 large eggplants	Mazola)

Clean or peel all vegetables and cut into small
pieces. Salt the vegetables and let stand for about one
half hour. Warm the oil and turn over the vegetables;
put them in a covered casserole. Steam about 3 hours in
the oven at a very low temperature. Can be served hot
or cold.

TABLE 1

IMMIGRATION OF ROMANIANS TO THE UNITED STATES

Period	No. of Immigrants
1871-1880	11
1881-1890	6,348
1891-1900	12,750
1901-1910	53,008
1911-1920	13,311
1921-1930	67,646
1931-1940	3,871
1941-1950	1,076
1951-1960	1,039
1961-1965	1,158
1966	242
1967	179
1968	214
1969	266
1970	472
1971	687
1972	354
1973	1,106
TOTAL 1820-1973	163,738

Source: United States Department of Justice. 1973 Annual Report Immigration and Naturalization Service. Washington, D. C.: U. S. Government Printing Office, 1973.

NOTE
     The above statistics have a relative value. Several thousands of Romanian immigrants resided in the United States temporarily, and then returned to their native country. On the other hand, the statistics recorded, besides Romanian stock, other ethnic groups such as Hungarians, Germans, Jews, Ukrainians, etc., who also emigrated from Romania but are beyond the scope of our study.

THE ROMANIANS IN AMERICA

TABLE 2

ROMANIAN STOCK IN THE U.S.A. BY NATIVITY AND RACE

Number	Percent Distribution
Total Romanian Stock	
Total - 216,803	0.6
White - 216,255	0.7
Foreign Born	
Total - 70,687	0.7
White - 70,364	0.8
Native of Foreign or Mixed Parentage	
Total - 146,116	0.6
White - 145,891	0.6

100% represents the entire foreign stock from all foreign countries. (33,575,232)

TABLE 3

ROMANIAN LANGUAGE DECLARED AS MOTHER TONGUE BY
NATIVITY, PARENTAGE AND RACE

	Total	White	Other races
Total	56,590	56,372	175
Native of Native Parentage	5,166	5,105	53
Native of Foreign or Mixed Parentage	25,369	25,928	92

Source: U. S. Department of Commerce. 1970 Census of Population; Detailed Characteristics - U. S. Summary. Washington, D. C.: U. S. Government Printing Office, 1973.